Contents

Part I: The Mighty Pray-er **1**
Becoming a Mighty Pray-er 3
Mighty Pray-ers 7
Answers for Mighty Pray-ers 15

Part II: The Mighty Prayers **31**
The Appreciation Prayer 33
The What Prayer 39
The Eternal Gratitude Prayer 47
The Image Prayer 53
The Five-Year Prayer 57
The Pulse Prayer 61
The Because Prayer 65
The Music Prayer 67
Mindful Prayers: Blessings on the Food 71

Part III: The Nonviolent Communication Prayer **77**
The Nonviolent Communication (NVC) Prayer: Introduction 79
The NVC Prayer in a Snapshot 83
The Four Steps 85
NVC Prayer Examples 111

Conclusion 115
Epilogue 117

Endnotes 119
About the Author 122

A Note to the Reader

Though there are three members of the Godhead, this book mostly focuses on only one: Heavenly Father. The first member of the Godhead is whom we address at the beginning of our prayers. The second member of the Godhead, Jesus Christ, is whom we end our prayer with. The third member of the Godhead, the Holy Ghost, conveys revelations from the Father and the Son.[1] All are vital to our spiritual growth, but the chapters of this book focus primarily on improving our relationship with Heavenly Father through communication with Him.

Because we address our prayer to Heavenly Father, it leads me to believe we are speaking directly to Him. Yet, we are taught that no unclean thing can be in the presence of God. So how does He receive our words? Do they travel the vast distance to Him? Or are there messenger angels who deliver the messages?

I don't know how it works, but I do know that I have had many experiences where I have felt I was in His presence. And as I've pondered on it, I've wondered if perhaps the cleansing power of the Atonement of Jesus Christ is what allows us to literally be in the presence of God while we speak to Him. This infinite Atonement permits us to encounter the Lord. Which means, you can encounter the Lord.

Are you ready?

Part I

The Mighty Pray-er

Becoming a Mighty Pray-er

My family's 2020 Easter celebration was a complete and utter disaster. Maybe it was because we had six children ages two to eleven. Or maybe it was because we had been homebound from COVID-19 for three weeks prior to that Sunday. Truthfully, it could have been due to a lack of preparation on my part. But with all the screaming and yelling and fighting and contention and disrupt, that Sabbath day was awful.

I was disheartened that night. We could have celebrated one of the most sacred and pivotal days of the year with beautiful and spiritual experiences, but instead we created terrible memories and probably lifelong trauma!

It was then, as my heart ached, that I gave my first mighty prayer. Sure, I'd said *a lot* of prayers before. I had even said a lot of "please-help-me-or-I-think-I'm-going-to-die" prayers. But never had I experienced a prayer like this—a prayer where I moved out of my head and into my heart and body.

This new prayer removed barriers of judgments and expectations I did not know I was living with. Because of this, it enlightened my mind to what my heart was truly feeling beneath surface emotions. It revealed to me an unfilled need I was yearning to satiate—that I wasn't even aware of. And all that was just my side of the prayer! That doesn't include the immediate answer I received from my Heavenly Father, which overfilled me with peace and direction.

I did not just happen to have a mighty prayer that night. I had been reading the book *Nonviolent Communication* by Marshall B. Rosenberg, which is about compassion and communication. And that night, I had the thought to pattern my prayer after the concepts taught in the book. I was tired of, what felt to me, one-sided prayers. I needed to pour out my soul and have a better conversation with God. The steps from *Nonviolent Communication* (applied to prayer later in this book) were the guide I needed.

President Gordon B. Hinckley said, "The trouble with most of our prayers is that we give them as if we were picking up the telephone and ordering groceries—we place our order and hang up. We need to meditate, contemplate, [and] think of what we are praying about and for."[2] Until that moment, most of my prayers were telephone orders or constant pleadings of "please help me, please help me, please help me." Even during my most difficult trials, I had prayed this way.

Furthermore, in trying to remain respectful and not demanding to the Great Almighty, my prayers often felt timid and bashful. "Uh, if You have time, uh, I could use help, but if not, uh, that's okay too. I totally get it," was the energy I would give.

But that Easter evening, following the impression to apply the steps of nonviolent communication to my prayer, my pleadings with the Lord shifted to expressing vulnerability and faith. This prayer took me inside my mind and my heart, and it illuminated things about myself I wasn't aware of. My relationship with Heavenly Father was strengthened, and I felt the Lord Jesus Christ heal me through His atoning power. I received an answer to my heartfelt, mighty prayer that night, and that answer brought me peace and direction.

This experience changed me. It opened my understanding to the possibility of sitting in the presence of my Father and talking *with* Him, not at Him. Because of this, I acquired a newfound awareness for encounters with the Great Divine.

In the Book of Mormon, Helaman—the leader of an army and a man of God—describes how his people did "pour out [their] souls in prayer to God, that he would strengthen [them] and deliver [them]." In the next verse, he says, "Yea, and it came to pass that the Lord our God did visit us with assurances that he would deliver us; yea, insomuch that *he did speak peace to our souls, and did grant unto us great faith, and did cause us that we should hope for our deliverance in him*."[3]

I was having a similar experience. I had poured out my soul to my Father and found faith, hope, and direction. I had created a space where I bonded with Him and strengthened our relationship. The outcome was peace to my soul, increased faith, and a solid, sure knowledge that Heavenly Father and His Son are our Deliverers. I had experienced my first mighty prayer.

This was the beginning of my discovery to pray more fully with heart and soul. Since then, I've tried new ways of praying. These ways, described throughout this book, help me to pray with more than just words. I've learned that truly communing with God—involving my physical senses and my heart—can nurture a relationship with my Father and bring about experiences I never thought I could have.

It can be that way for you too.

If indeed the quality of our lives is largely a product of the kinds of associations we enjoy, then we may rest assured that individuals who spend much time in prayer will in time blossom in personality, rise above pettiness, littleness of soul, and mortal jealousies and fears.

—ROBERT L. MILLET

Mighty Pray-ers

We have many examples of mighty pray-ers in the scriptures, and, by observing them, we witness the results of a mighty prayer. One example is the young prophet Joseph Smith. In 1820, Joseph Smith, at age fourteen, experienced inner conflict. Not knowing which church to attend, he desired knowledge and direction. He sent a heartfelt prayer heavenward and communed with Heavenly Father and Jesus Christ.[4] The Church of Jesus Christ of Latter-day Saints on the earth today is the result of the efforts of this mighty, effortful prayer.

Not only did Joseph's mighty prayer change lives worldwide, but it also changed Joseph's personal relationship with God. Truman G. Madsen said, "In the modern prophet Joseph Smith we have an example of living, breathing prayer—the kind that changes life. His early successes with prayer were the foundation of a pattern that brought him progressively closer to God."[5] Joseph Smith's relationship with Heavenly Father exemplifies the possibilities of communing.

Other examples of mighty pray-ers can be found in the Book of Mormon. In fact, the first story in this special, sacred record is about a mighty pray-er and the results of his prayer. Lehi, the father of Nephi, went forth and "prayed unto the Lord, yea, even with all his heart."[6] After this heartfelt and mighty prayer, a pillar of fire appeared before him, and he "saw and heard much."[7] He connected with the heavens, and his prayer was answered.

Enos, another Book of Mormon prophet and mighty pray-er, is often one of the first to come to mind on the topic of prayer. He recognized his soul was hungering, and he acted on this feeling by supplicating himself before the Lord all day, all night, and even into the next day. Enos poured out his whole soul to the Lord—he found that space inside himself of vulnerability, longing, suffering, and desire, and he opened it to the Lord to heal. He "pray[ed] unto him with many long strugglings" and "labor[ed] with all diligence."[8] Finally, after this mighty prayer was offered up and the Lord communed with him, his "soul did rest."[9] Enos strengthened his relationship with the Lord and found solace and comfort.

Alma the Younger is also a great example of mighty praying. He "labored much in the spirit, wrestling with God in mighty prayer, that he would pour out his Spirit upon the people who were in the city."[10] These words imply that Alma was not just speaking from his mind, but he was communing with God from his heart. His whole soul was involved in the pleadings with God. He "wrestled" with the Lord. A friend of mine, a mother of national champion wrestlers, once told me that wrestling uses every muscle in your body. What kind of prayer did Alma have if he used his whole heart, soul, *and* every muscle in his body? Seeing how wrestling also needs an opponent, or a partner, this word also indicates Alma was having an up-close and personal experience with the Lord. Mighty prayers are personal experiences with our Father, nurturing our relationship with Him.

This is what a mighty pray-er does: they seek a relationship with the Lord through the vehicle of prayer. It is *you* who opens your soul and allows your Father deeper into the crevices of your hidden spaces. It is the employment of your physical senses and the expansion of your inner realm in expression, resulting in a closer relationship with the Great God Almighty, the Father of your spirit. Authors of *The Power of Stillness: Mindful Living for Latter-day Saints* wrote, "Thoughtful, mindful, reverent prayer is about cultivating a relationship with God as a real Being to whom we can speak genuinely, intimately, and personally."[11] A mighty pray-er draws closer to God and facilitates a more intimate relationship with Him through communing.

Mighty pray-ers nurture their relationship with God, just like they nurture their relationships with other people. One way we improve relationships with others is by having shared experiences. Another way is through physical touch and affection. We can also nurture relationships by improving ourselves—by evaluating who we are and how to work better with others. As a parent, I build relationships with my children in these ways. I spend time having shared experiences with them. I offer my love through hugs and encouraging touch. I also strive to improve myself by molding my heart and expectations so I can work better with each child's needs and differences.

Just as it takes effort to build relationships with our children, our spouse, our siblings, and others in our lives, similar effort is required to foster and build a relationship with Heavenly Father and Jesus Christ. We need to spend time with Them, have shared experiences with Them, and be present with Them. Since we can't have physical touch with God, we can be aware of our physical senses when we are praying, reading the scriptures, or being thoughtful about impressions from Heavenly Father as we receive them. For example, what does it feel like on the skin of your arms after you pray and invite the spirit to answer your prayers? In addition to this, we also must be willing to learn to mold our hearts and expectations, expand our abilities to love Them differently than how we naturally do, and forgive Them when our expectations are not met. This book is a compilation of ways to do this.

I love this example of a modern-day mighty pray-er. Her name is Callie, and she is a senior in high school. She recently shared this in our stake conference:

> I've found that when I'm most overwhelmed is the time when the spirit *begs* me to turn to Christ instead of me trying to handle it alone. How do I do it though? How do I move past my worldly thoughts and reach out to a Heavenly Being for help? I think about this all the time and here's what I've got.
>
> So when I have questions or desperately need someone to talk to, I actually go to the window in my room, often in the middle of the night, with all the lights off, and I pray *out loud* to Heavenly Father. The calming sounds of the night and seeing the beautiful stars brings me so much joy. And with the peace I feel from praying to Heavenly Father, it's hard to imagine a time I will ever feel greater than I do sitting next to my window—because that's the time I finally give up, and let the Lord help me.
>
> I know sitting next to a window sounds odd, but I've found a place where I can feel the spirit and know that when I turn

> to Christ I will not be turned away. My experience praying by my window is not exactly like Joseph's experience in the sacred grove: I don't see Heavenly Father and Jesus. They don't come down and speak to me. But I feel their presence, and I know they're there. And usually that's all I need.[12]

I love how Callie spent intentional time with Heavenly Father, using her physical senses to be present and aware of her surroundings and to strengthen her relationship with Him. This is a beautiful example of a mighty prayer.

I recently participated in a Prophetic Heart Healing training found online at www.prophetichearthealing.com. Elise Tarango, trainer and co-founder of the program, said, "Real relationships include shared life experiences together. Conversations."[13] That is the purpose of the mighty prayer. The prayers suggested in this book are simple ways to express your heart and draw nearer to Him, increase your faith and rely more on His strength, and enhance your experiences encountering Heavenly Father. These prayers are a way to have conversations with the Lord, a way to have a shared experience with Him.

Not only is our emotional connection to Heavenly Father important when we pray, but our literal connection is vital to keep in mind. I love Elder David A. Bednar's insight on this: "Prayer becomes meaningful as we remember our relationship to Deity."[14] Heavenly Father is the literal father of our spirit. How might our prayers change if we remember this when we approach Him, desiring to deepen our relationship, and spend intentional time creating a shared experience?

As it may now seem obvious, a mighty pray-er does *not* pray with the Lord to get what he or she wants. The purpose of this book is not to learn to change the will of God, for changing the will of God and getting what you want is not the miracle of a mighty prayer. At a fireside in 2002, Virginia H. Pearce said, "The miracle of prayer does not reside in the ability to manipulate situations and events."[15] The miracle of the mighty prayer is to soften the natural man in yourself and move closer to God, thus creating a deeper relationship with Him. The miracle is that He is God and we are man, and we can still have a relationship with Him.

I appreciated the way Angela Montano described prayer in a welcome email after I signed up for her course, 21 Days of Prayer to Change Your Life. In comparing prayer and meditation, she said the following:

> What prayer and meditation have in common is that both involve a "turning within." When we turn within to meditate, we are interested in space, in growing more conscious by seeing the activity of our thoughts and emotions. We are the witnesses. When we meditate, we are seeing the duality of our thinking, but we are not trying to "fix" this. Instead, we are simply watching and gaining awareness. This is a powerful spiritual practice that more and more people are doing all over the world.
>
> When we pray, while we are still "turning within," it is quite different. Through prayer, we are laying down our fears, doubts, and worries, and delivering our painful perceptions to this greater power within us. In prayer, we are choosing change. We are choosing release from suffering. We are surrendering the dualistic mind to the "one" mind.
>
> When we pray for a moment, even for a second, it is an act of faith. In that instance, something within us opens to the possibility of freedom from suffering. We open ourselves to the higher power of our own understanding to change us and the situation we associate with our pain or the pain of others.[16]

That is the miracle of prayer. It is the expression of faith, a moment of raw vulnerability, an opportunity for healing and growth, and the connection to something greater than ourselves. It is a transcendent experience. At least it can be.

I learned a valuable lesson about the importance of being connected in such an intimate way to something bigger early on in my marriage and as a mom. When my husband was in graduate school, we had two small children and no income. The fact that we had no income meant that our daughters could attend a federally funded early-education program for families with limited financial resources.

While these were difficult times for us, this educational program was a great blessing to our family and girls.

One of the most meaningful parent-child benefits came through the integration of a program called Circle of Security. Circle of Security is an attachment theory that helps parents and other caregivers to follow children's relationship needs, to then understand those needs, and to know how to become more emotionally available to their children. The process and steps in Circle of Security are often demonstrated with a visual representation of a child's physical journey of exploration away from and then returning to his or her parent. In this diagram, there are two hands which represent the parent as the child's safe base. Then it shows a circle leading away from and returning to the hands. This circle represents the child leaving the secure base to go out and explore, play, learn, and grow, and then coming back to check in or have needs met.[17]

John Bowlby, the father of attachment theory, said, "Intimate attachments to other human beings are the hub around which a person's life revolves, not only as an infant or a toddler or a schoolchild but throughout adolescence and years of maturity as well, and on into old age. From these intimate attachments a person draws strength and enjoyment of life and, through what he contributes, gives strength and enjoyment to others."[18] If you have an intimate and secure attachment to the safe hands in your life, you can draw strength in times of need and feel a deeper sense of fulfillment and joy. You can also provide strength and joy to others.

You might wonder if you have this kind of support in your life. You might wonder if you are providing that attachment to your children. You might wonder if your parents or your spouse is that secure base for you. Whether or not you have those hands in your life, we all have one common set of hands we can always come back to—our Heavenly Father's. He is our eternal, constant, secure base. I think of this often when I hear the phrase "return and report." Perhaps we are encouraged to return and report because that is the natural cycle of our attachment need. Each day, we go out on our circle, exploring, learning, growing, making mistakes, needing help, needing Him to watch over us, delight in us, protect us, and comfort us. He invites us back to that safe, secure base. Our moments in prayer provide that returning to Him. They allow us to refill our love-cup through the one true source of unlimited love. They allow us to draw strength and enjoyment in life through this intimate attachment. What an incredible thing!

Now, there are a myriad of ways to have your own mighty prayer. This book explores a limited number, introducing the Appreciation Prayer, the What Prayer, the Eternal Gratitude Prayer, the Image Prayer, the Five-Year Prayer, the Pulse Prayer, the Because Prayer, the Music Prayer, the Mindful Blessing Prayer, and the Nonviolent Communication (NVC) Prayer. Each of these prayers has a different way to be present in your body, access your heart, and guide you to pray with your "heart, might, mind, and strength."[19] Try each one out a few times. I wonder what changes you will see in your life and in your relationship with your Father.

God is approachable, generous, and willing to answer our prayers.

—JOHN BYTHEWAY

Answers for Mighty Pray-ers

One of the blessings of a mighty prayer is the experiences during and after the prayer—sometimes *immediately* after. Answers, enlightenment, shifts in perspective, and feelings can come. The Lord God wants to commune! Emily Belle Freeman, the Young Women General President, wrote, "Praying constantly allows us to have an on-going conversation with the Lord. When we pray frequently throughout the day and address specific needs, we open the door to receive *more frequent and specific answers.*"[20] We can receive answers to our mighty prayers. I have believed this my entire life, but only in recent years have I lived this. And I know others who have lived it too.

Tarango said, "When I first encountered [God] it was a major revelation to me to learn that He wanted to speak with me. That He wanted to have those direct conversations. It wasn't listing off my laundry list to Him. But it was a real living active conversation with Him." She continued: "It starts with hearing [God's] voice."[21] It takes practice to hear His answers, to "hear Him."[22] And practice involves not just listening but being in tune to our physical senses and recognizing how God communicates with us individually. Tarango describes different ways we can hear Him. She says, "A thought. Words. A scripture. A picture or image. Notice a change in the way you are seeing or sensing something. Everyone hears and encounters the Lord differently."[23] Similarly, David Butler, a college religious instructor and author, writes, "Elijah got a whisper, and Moses got a flame."[24]

Jessica Garner, a friend who is journeying to hear Him, writes about a time she was unsure of an impression from Heavenly Father but trusted it anyway.

> I recently went on a family vacation to California. It was a beautiful trip, but the night before we had to leave, I felt very sad that I hadn't been able to spend more time in the ocean: a place I love but rarely get to experience. The plan for the last day was for everyone to work together to pack and prepare the rental house for check out, then travel to the beach one more time before flying home.
>
> My heart ached to put my feet in the sand and waves one more time, before we had to leave. It was really important to me.
>
> Well, on our last day, my baby had me up before everyone else in the house, so I carried him to the back porch to look at the ocean. I was about to do a meditation that begins with prayer. During my opening prayer, I noticed that I accidentally imagined myself walking the nearby beach. At first, I thought I was just daydreaming or distracted. I said to myself, "I don't think it's the safest of beaches, and there isn't enough time to visit the water before it'll be time to pack." However, I also had been learning to trust my thoughts. When I imagine myself doing something, I accept it as possibly a thought from God.
>
> So I prayed, "Heavenly Father, I think that thought came from You, so I'll walk the beach. Thank you."
>
> I wrapped Baby into a blanket and walked down to the beach!
>
> It was a lovely, peaceful walk for me that entirely filled my deep desire to put my feet in the ocean again. I was so grateful.
>
> Fast forward through the rest of the beautiful morning, to where circumstances changed which caused us to not be able to visit a beach before we had to fly away! Now, as I write, tears of gratitude are in my eyes as I consider Heavenly Father's love for me and my little desire to visit the ocean. I'm so grateful He sent me a little message during my prayer and that I trusted myself.[25]

How often might we receive images or ideas in our mind right in the middle of praying? How often do we dismiss them in an attempt to stay focused on our prayer? Might some of these images or impressions be nudges from our Heavenly Father? What might happen if we consider this and act on them?

How does God communicate with you? Do you see images in your mind's eye? Do you hear words in your mind's ears? Do you think thoughts that don't feel like your own? Do you notice subtle shifts in the way you are feeling? Or sense something different after a prayer? Do messages from Heavenly Father come as physical sensations through your gut or your back? Your neck or your spine? Once I began believing that subtle shifts in the way I felt were actually answers from above, I began receiving more and more. How will awareness increase your trust and belief that you can receive answers? Elder Alexander Dushku, a General Authority Seventy, gives us other examples of how the Lord communicates with us:

> Every one of us is different. No two people experience God's light and truth in exactly the same way. Take some time to think about how you experience the light and Spirit of the Lord.
>
> You may have experienced these bursts of light and testimony as "peace [spoken] to your mind concerning [a] matter" that has worried you.
>
> Or as an impression—a still, small voice—that settled "in your mind and in your heart" and urged you to do something good, such as helping someone.
>
> Perhaps you've been in a class at church—or at a youth camp—and felt a strong desire to follow Jesus Christ and stay faithful. Maybe you even stood and shared a testimony that you hoped was true and then felt it was.
>
> Or maybe you've been praying and felt a joyful assurance that God loves you.
>
> You may have heard someone bear testimony of Jesus Christ, and it touched your heart and filled you with hope.
>
> Perhaps you were reading in the Book of Mormon and a verse spoke to your soul, as if God had put it there just for you—and then you realized that He did.

> You may have felt the love of God for others as you served them.
>
> Or maybe you struggle to feel the Spirit in the moment because of depression or anxiety but have the precious gift and the faith to look back and recognize past "tender mercies of the Lord."
>
> There are many ways to receive heavenly rays of testimony.[26]

Do you resonate with any of these examples? Can you list all the different ways you have recognized hearing Him in your life? As you try out some of the prayers suggested in this book, I wonder what other ways God will speak to you as you experience mighty prayers.

Allie Duzett is a member of The Church of Jesus Christ of Latter-day Saints and a medical intuitive, one who uses intuition to promote healing and wellness. In her practice of learning to sense her intuition, she has also learned to recognize the subtle voice of God on a more regular basis. She shares an insightful perspective on how Heavenly Father communicates to us through our physical bodies.

> We have to practice experiencing [revelation] in our own physical bodies. This is how God speaks to humans. Within the vessel of their physical form. This is how we experience it. You do it in your body. There's lots of scriptures that say you'll recognize the voice of God because of that burning in your bosom. Which is a feeling that you feel in your physical body. . . . Our physical bodies are the vehicle for feeling the feelings of revelation.[27]

If you are still learning how God speaks to you, pay attention to Butler's suggestion. "One of the best pieces of advice someone ever gave me when learning to recognize the Spirit was to ask God for help. Ask Him to help you learn the way He speaks to you."[28] Heavenly Father wants you to learn how to hear Him, and He can teach you! Ask Him to make it obvious. Ask Him to heighten your awareness of His voice. Duzett encourages:

> Ask for a training program! Ask God for help in practicing feeling the Holy Spirit in low stakes situations. It takes the pressure off yourself. "God, send me a situation today where I can practice feeling the Holy Spirit in a low stakes environment so if I mess up, it's no big deal. But I'll have the chance to do something good or whatever, and either way, it won't be a big deal."[29]

Ponder for a moment. How do you hear Him? How do you receive His messages to you? If you aren't sure, ask for a training program to learn to hear His voice. This awareness is vital and possible. Elder Richard G. Scott said, "I witness that as you gain experience and success in being guided by the Spirit, your confidence in the impressions you feel can become more certain than your dependence on what you see or hear."[30] What might change in your life if you ask Heavenly Father to teach you how He speaks to you?

Improving our ability to hear Him improves our relationship with Him. Hank R. Smith, professor of religion at Brigham Young University–Provo, said, "A portion of my dissertation for my doctoral degree was spent researching listening. If you want to improve every relationship in your life, practice listening."[31]

Often our environment is so loud and full of commotion that it is hard to hear Him. Heavenly Father does not compete to be heard and sensed above all this noise. Rather, He uses quiet and stillness. To recognize His presence, we must often work to tune out the world around us and then to calm our inner world—our thoughts. Just as I would turn down the radio to listen to my daughter, we must also turn down the volume to have a conversation with God. As we do this, communication becomes more clear, and we recognize Him better. "The quieter we become, the more we can hear," the poet Rumi wrote.[32]

Preparing Our Inner Environment to Hear Him

How can we calm our inner environment? Authors of *The Power of Stillness* suggest taking a few minutes of silence before praying. "We have found that a short period of intentional silence helps sharpen our focus for what follows, allowing us to take into our prayer an attunement of the ear and willingness to listen."[33] Dedicating a few moments—or even minutes—before praying to sit in stillness helps you quiet your inner environment.

I find it very difficult to just sit in silence. My mind races, and it's hard to stop thinking about all the things that need to get done. So training my mind to focus and notice what's happening in my body is a helpful way to sit in stillness. You can try this right now! Tune into your body by becoming aware of your physical senses. Close your eyes and take a few normal breaths. Focus on the rim of your nostrils. What does it feel like as air passes into your nose? What does it feel like as your chest rises and falls with each breath? Now ask yourself, "What do I smell?" Try to identify scents in the air. Then ask yourself, "What can I feel?" Reach out with your fingers and touch your nose or your hair. Touch the beveled edges of a zipper, the smoothness of a button, or the cotton weavings of your shoelace. Notice what it feels like on your fingertips to touch those things. Then ask yourself, "What can I taste?" Run your tongue over your teeth for any flavors. Anything lingering from dinner? Maybe a hint of minty toothpaste? Now ask yourself, "What can I see?" But before opening your eyes, imagine that everything you see will be looking back at you. Then slowly open your eyes and look around. Sit in this moment to "be seen" by the objects around you. This exercise can bring your body and spirit into the present moment. I love the way I feel after doing this exercise.

And I feel more ready to tune into my mind and thoughts. To do this, close your eyes again and imagine your mind is a room full of words representing your thoughts and ideas. Imagine seeing a broom sweeping your mind clean of thoughts. Your list of to-do's are spread like dust balls across the floor. Your worries and stresses are strung about like cobwebs. Take the broom to them all until they are swept to a corner where you can return to them when you have finished conversing with God. Calm your mind to the best of your ability. New thoughts and ideas will enter the room, but when you recognize they have taken your attention, sweep them away again.

Once you have swept your mind empty a few times, draw your focus to your heart. Consider placing your hands over your sternum, the flat bone in the center of your chest where your ribs meet. Spend a few moments thanking your heart for sustaining your life. Allow yourself to feel any emotions. Sometimes, by bringing awareness to my heart, I realize it's been carrying sadness for a while, or maybe frustration and anger. Notice the emotions that arise, acknowledge them, and sit with them. If you feel the need, explore them a little more. Sometimes our hearts notify us of what we need to mightily pray about—something our minds are not consciously aware of. When you feel ready, you can move into your mighty prayer.

Being mindful of what is going on in our bodies, our minds, and our hearts is preparatory to a mighty prayer. Mindful awareness is referred to as "mindfulness." "Mindfulness is simply awareness—the skill of being aware of what's happening inside and around you: thoughts, feelings, physical sensations, and what the traditional five senses notice about the tangible world. This is an awareness of what's unfolding in the present moment, without overanalyzing the past or predicting the future."[34] Mindfulness allows us to be fully present in our conversation with the Lord. It also heightens our awareness to the subtle answers and shifts in our bodies, minds, and hearts as a result of prayer. This allows for an ongoing conversation with the Lord that nurtures our relationship and fosters love.

What if sweeping all the thoughts and distractions away doesn't quiet the inner world? Is it possible to *stop thinking*? Can we really shut off our thoughts and have an empty mind? Author Jacob Hess said, "Many who step off the treadmills of their lives to cultivate more stillness do, in fact, initially experience a sense of slowing down and calm. But then, almost universally, people start to notice surprising levels of distracting emotions and 'chatter' in the mind."[35] This is normal. Expect it. Sweep it away, then sweep it away again. And then sweep it away one more time. Heavenly Father will take note of your efforts and your determination to commune with Him. "The Lord loves effort."[36] He will see your soul's wrestle with "many long strugglings." He will notice your "labor with all diligence."[37] And He will listen and respond.

Challenge: Before your next prayer, set a timer for three minutes and sit in stillness. Ask yourself what you are experiencing through your physical senses. Take note and focus your attention on each of your five senses. Spend time there. Then visualize your mind as a room and sweep your thoughts into the corner, a garbage bin, or a cabinet to pull out and mull over later. Sweep it all away until you can see an empty room and sit in stillness. When your mind wanders or new thoughts enter the room, recognize them, and then sweep them away too. After three minutes, reset the alarm and visualize going to your heart and feeling the emotions there. Explore them, or just let them be. Sit with them until the time is up.

Then begin your mighty prayer.

Addressing Unanswered Prayers

But what happens after you do all this and then no answers come? What do you do when you don't feel, see, or hear answers from the Lord?

I have felt this way many times. When I was pregnant with my seventh baby, I felt the heavens grow quiet. During that pregnancy, I struggled to hear His answers and the promptings of the Holy Ghost. It was a lonely, difficult time. I wondered, had I done something to deserve the silence? Did I not matter to Heavenly Father? Or were the heavens quiet because Heavenly Father wanted me to make my own decisions? Was it because I had not acted on previous promptings and was experiencing chastisement? Was it because I wasn't asking the right questions? Was it something I was doing? Was I not praying "hard enough"? Was I receiving answers but not recognizing them? Was I not worthy? I was bewildered without any clue as to why the heavens were quiet.

I could relate to what Angie Asplund, the face behind @healthful_dwelling, wrote:

> Connecting with the Divine wasn't always easy for me. Receiving answers and guidance seemed hard. I thought those answers and guidance had to come in a certain way. I thought I had to just go about life and wait for said answers to come to me. I would ask and then wait as if I was an object waiting to be acted upon. As if I had no control of when the answers came. Not true. Not true. Not true. I was wrong.[38]

Angie explains how she now understands the answers she receives. She said, "Want to know my secret? Filling my toolbox with ways I can receive answers. God will answer you in any way you are open to. So fill your toolbox." Angie describes multiple ways she receives divine answers: prayer journaling, flipping open her scriptures, muscle testing (a method of tapping into the subconscious mind using muscles of the body), listening to the first words that come to her mind, [and] noticing the feelings in her body (no feels different than yes).[39]

What tools are in your toolbox? What ways has the Lord answered you that might be overlooked because they are different than you expected?

Recognizing False Beliefs We Have About God

Emily Robison Adams, author of *Divine Quietness*, describes her journey of when the heavens felt shut to her. She shares another perspective about how her years of divine quietness challenged her to expand her understanding of God and how He communicates with her. "I had a core belief that God would respond in a certain way if I followed particular steps; when I felt [angry from not receiving answers in a way I could recognize], I wanted to hold onto that belief with a tight fist, ignoring the experience I was having."[40] After months and years of painful struggles feeling angry, alone, betrayed, and depressed, she began to peel back layers of untrue beliefs about God. This has been an ongoing process for her. She writes, "The purpose of the quietness is to help us realize and then release our small ideas about God. It can also help us approach our spiritual life differently: instead of obeying the commandments or engaging in spiritual practices because we expect something from them, we obey and engage simply because we love."[41]

Adams expresses: "I am learning to view divine quietness as a refining experience, as a tool God uses to clear out notions that clutter and weaken faith through the painful process of riveting my attention on what I wanted most but could not find: God."[42] Ultimately, Adams used this time to strengthen her relationship with her Father. By uncovering and cleansing limiting beliefs about Him, and discovering who His character truly is, she was able to gain a relationship with a real Divine Being, rather than struggle with an image of Him she had created in her mind. "I can see the possibility that God can go quiet. But a quiet God is not an angry God or a careless God or an arbitrary God. I can see that quietness can be an invitation to a deeper look at myself and at my relationship with God."[43] I love Sister Tracy Browning's words from the 2024 October general conference: "We may be required to 'wait upon the Lord' in the space between our current line of understanding and the next yet to be delivered. This sacred space can be a place where our greatest spiritual conditioning can occur—the site where we can 'bear with patience' our earnest seeking and renew our strength to continue to keep the sacred promises we have made to God through covenant."[44] This refining and conditioning silence can help us rededicate our lives to God's laws and covenants while we "[w]ait on the Lord."[45] So "[b]e of good courage, and he shall strengthen thine heart. Wait, I say, on the Lord."[46]

If you are experiencing divine quietness in your life right now, ponder on the following questions over the next few minutes. Ask them out loud, and see what thoughts come to your mind.

- What has my past led me to believe about prayer?
- Might there be limiting expectations in the way of who I think God is?
- Do I have false expectations of how He communicates with me?

W. Paul Reeve, author of *Let's Talk About Race and Priesthood,* quotes Dieter F. Uchtdorf: "How often has the Holy Spirit tried to tell us something we needed to know but couldn't get past the massive iron gate of what we thought we already knew?" Reeve then follows Uchtdorf's statement by saying, "Letting go of past assumptions can be unsettling, but it can also invite new insights and lift our vision to new heights. For me, the journey has not been easy, and my heart has sometimes broken under the strain of it—and it sometimes still does."[47] Limiting, untrue beliefs can prevent us from recognizing the abundance of divine guidance available to us. This quiet time might be an opportunity for you to uncover some of your unhealthy, limiting beliefs about His nature and character. Or it might be a time to discover and cleanse your motives for obeying and communing with Him. Can you discern any you might be holding onto?

How to Get Rid of Limiting Beliefs

If limiting, untrue beliefs reside in your subconscious, then it feels incongruent and a strain to believe anything else. How can you receive revelation if deep inside you believe you must be "righteous enough" for God to talk to you? If your subconscious believes God only answers those He loves, and if you don't feel you're receiving answers, then might your subconscious conclude He does not love you? Can you see how detrimental limiting beliefs are? That is why it is so crucial to learn to identify these beliefs and get rid of them.

The problem, though, with limiting beliefs is that they reside in your subconscious mind, and you often don't know they are there. They are tricky to recognize! How can you even identify them? Let's explore this.

I asked a group of people to share their limiting beliefs around prayers being answered. Their responses hurt my heart, and I found myself painfully aware that I have felt the same way. Can you relate to any of these?

- I have to be good enough for God to answer me.
- I'm not good enough.
- I don't deserve God to answer me.
- Only others deserve God's answers.
- I don't feel a burning, get tingles, or feel the Spirit.
- I often talk myself out of hearing Him by saying, "Oh, that was just my own thought, not inspiration."
- God will ask for more than I'm willing to give, so I'm afraid of hearing His answers.
- If God cared enough about me to hear my prayers, then He wouldn't have let my life be this awful.
- Revelation and answers come a specific way, and since I don't receive this specific way, I'm not receiving answers.
- If He doesn't answer my prayers, then I must have done something wrong.

- God doesn't speak to me (or at least I don't know *how* He speaks to me).
- Others have the gift of hearing Him; I do not.
- I fail at prayer because I don't do it right (i.e., not on my knees, forget to do "morning" prayer and end up praying at noon, etc.).
- I have to do all I can before I can involve God.
- I have to do all that I can before God will help me.
- I have to have it all worked out before God can answer me.
- I have to struggle for answers.
- I have to work hard for answers.
- God doesn't care about these trivial issues in my life.
- Deep inside, I'm afraid God is going to tell me something I don't want to hear/do/experience, which takes my agency out of the equation. For example, praying if there are "more children waiting for our family" when I don't want to be pregnant again.
- Something is wrong with me that I'm not understanding the answer.
- I need to speak amazing words for God to hear my prayers.
- I am dumb or spiritually deaf because I don't recognize the answer or have an answer that makes any sense to me.
- Prayer always has to be formal, in a certain format.
- The things I pray for are "not His will," so I preemptively decide I'm not going to get them anyway.
- I'll never see the answers.
- God is always mysterious.
- It's hard to understand God.
- I am afraid to hear God.
- God requires too much.
- God is too busy for someone like me.
- I don't deserve God's time or attention.
- God doesn't hear me.
- I can't bother God with my cares.
- God only talks to prophets.
- He only hears my prayers when I'm praying for someone else.
- I just have to get what I get, so why bother to even ask?
- When I ask for blessings, I get trials.

- I feel unworthy to receive my desires.
- I feel my desires are dumb or not righteous enough so I won't get them.
- If I pray for something, I'll get a different blessing.
- What I want involves others, so I'm not going to get it.
- I don't know how to not want specific outcomes.
- My wants and desires are low on the totem pole.
- I've messed up too many times to be answered, especially when I know better.
- I'm too flawed to receive answers.
- I have sins I don't want to give up, so why would Heavenly Father answer my prayers?
- I don't know how to hear Him.
- I can't do it right.
- I can't hear God.
- God doesn't talk to me.[48]

What do you think of these limiting beliefs? Do you resonate with any of them? Are you ready to release one right now?

Because of the power of the Atonement of Jesus Christ, it is possible to release limiting beliefs that plague us. It is a simple process, and once the beliefs are gone, then you can embrace and believe truth. There are three main steps to releasing unhealthy beliefs: 1) recognize the unhealthy belief, 2) imagine pulling it out of your spirit and body, and 3) insert a new, true belief. Let's do it right now.

Step 1: Ask yourself right now—actually say these words out loud—"What limiting beliefs do I have around prayer?" Don't let your conscious, intellectual mind answer. Wait a moment and let those deep beliefs surface. See what comes to you.

If you're still unsure, go ahead and pick one that you resonated with from the list above. There may be more than one that you'd like to release, but just do one at a time.

Step 2: Imagine your limiting belief is written on an old movie reel in your brain. Now, visualize grabbing the end and unrolling that reel. Watch it unwind like an old cassette tape. Visualize pulling it through your body. Pull, pull, pull. Let it unwind, and watch it pull out of all areas of your body—your toes, your organs, your cells, your atoms, and your spirit body. Watch it pile up outside of your brain. Pull and pull until the tape comes off the reel and the reel is empty. Now imagine you are handing that giant pile of tape over to the Savior. When He takes it, it dissolves in His hands. Every last trace of that limiting belief is gone. He has taken it, borne it, and met the requisites of justice. You are free. You can now take a deep breath in as a new creature.[49]

Step 3: Now you can replace your limiting belief with true, healthy beliefs. I like to do this while tapping my forehead or my collarbone. Tapping helps scramble the energy that contained my unhealthy belief and inputs the new one. You can tap fast, or you can tap slow. The speed doesn't matter. It might feel awkward or embarrassing, but no one is watching and judging you. Try it out!

When coming up with healthy truths, it can be hard for your subconscious to believe a complete opposite right away. For example, if I released, "I am not good enough for God to answer me," and then I say the opposite, "I am good enough for God to answer me," my subconscious might fight it and reject it because it is so drastically opposing what I have believed and held onto for so long. But if you begin phrases with the word(s) like "maybe" and "some people," it is more convincing and acceptable. I also like to move into "I don't know how I can, but I can . . ." phrases, and end with the final truth that I now want to believe and accept with my whole being.

For example, I would tap and say all of these out loud, three times, in order:

- "Some people are good enough to get answers from God."
- "Some people are not good enough to get answers from God, but they still do."
- "Maybe I am good enough to receive answers from God."
- "Maybe I am not good enough, but maybe I can still receive answers from God."
- "Maybe I don't have to be good enough to receive answers."
- "Maybe I can receive answers regardless of whether I'm good enough or not."
- "I don't know how I can, but I can receive answers from God."
- "I don't know how I will do it, but I can receive answers from God whether I am good enough or not."

- "I am capable of receiving answers from God."
- "I can receive answers from God."

I complete this by taking a couple deep breaths.

There was a time when I held a limiting belief that it was easier for Heavenly Father to answer others' prayers than my own. I attended Ricks College in the last two years of its existence, and then attended BYU–Idaho for another two years and graduated with my bachelor's degree. During this time, I prayed to my best ability, but my limiting belief prevented me from witnessing the miracle of answered prayers. I had faith He would answer, but I didn't know anything about limiting beliefs, and I didn't know I was harboring one.

During my sophomore year, I had the idea to keep a prayer journal. Every time I was done praying, I would record all of my requests. After a while, this habit faded as there seemed to be no benefit in continuing.

Almost twenty years later, and after great efforts in releasing a myriad of limiting beliefs, I found the journal tucked away in storage. When I began scanning the pages, I was able to see that all my pleas had been answered. Not immediately, and not always in the way I had hoped or expected, but I could see God's hand in my life. I didn't get the A on the test that I had prayed for, but I passed the class and kept my scholarship, which was my ultimate desire in that prayer. My friend's challenging relationship was now happy and blossoming. My pleadings to understand certain gospel topics had been addressed only a few short years later. As I read my journal and looked back over my life, my heart felt warmth and an expansion of God's love, as well as a greater understanding of His involvement in my life. He had heard my prayers and answered them. I could see it so clearly now, and I wondered how my life could have been different without that and other limiting beliefs.

Our caring Heavenly Father wants to communicate with us. As we work to quiet our outer and inner environment, and cleanse our unhealthy and limiting beliefs, we can truly encounter Him. We can strengthen our relationship with Him. We can feel His love and His presence in our physical bodies. And we can be strengthened on our journey through life.

Part II

The Mighty Prayers

The rest of this book is a collection of different ways I have prayed over the past few years in my ongoing journey to becoming a mighty prayer. These are my mighty prayer techniques, and I share them with you in hopes you'll try them out and have your own unique, wonderful experiences with Heavenly Father. I also hope they spark new ideas in you to find your own ways to add depth and relationship in your mighty prayers. With a heart and mind open for new communication techniques and a willingness to accept His will however it might come, your mighty prayers will bring beautiful, enriching experiences to your life. I'm excited for you.

The Appreciation Prayer

The traditional common prayer heard throughout families, youth activities, and church meetings follows a simple Primary song suggestion: "I begin by saying 'Dear Heavenly Father'; I thank him for blessings he sends; Then humbly I ask him for things that I need, In the name of Jesus Christ, Amen."[50] This is the pattern for prayer that many people default to when praying. We begin by opening the prayer to Heavenly Father, we list off some things we are grateful for, we ask for help in what we need, and then we close in the name of Jesus Christ. This is not a bad thing, but when it becomes rote and habitual, I believe we miss out on the opportunity to strengthen our relationship with Heavenly Father.

In the book of John, we read about the Savior's prayer when His dear friend Lazarus dies. This prayer begins the way we are taught in song, but it does not feel rote or habitual. It feels heartfelt and genuine. We can learn from His example.

John records the first words Jesus Christ prays: "Father, I thank thee that thou hast heard me."[51] He starts off by giving thanks, but what does He give thanks for? He *preemptively* thanks His Heavenly Father for listening to Him. Have you ever started your prayer by thanking Heavenly Father for listening to what you are about to say? How might your experience change if you did? What might it feel like in your body and senses if you did this?

Some of my most powerful healing moments are when a friend listens to me. You know—truly listens. No judgments are made, and the listener doesn't try to solve my problems. They just offer their presence and sit and listen. This kind of friend is valuable and rare. But this is what we can experience with God every time we pray! He offers His presence and sits and listens. We can preemptively give thanks for that as we begin our prayer.

Just today as I was starting my prayer this way, I had the thought to give thanks for *all* my prayers He has listened to. I thought of the past forty years of my life—the prayers at my bedside, the whispered ones during intense moments, the wordless ones on my heart during tragedies. *All* of them. I felt humbled as I realized my own Father has listened to every single one of them. In my body, I felt a deep warmth at my core. It was a sweet moment.

I love that the Savior exemplified beginning His prayer by giving thanks. Starting our prayers with thanks is an incredibly powerful way to pray. My understanding of this importance expanded during the Prophetic Heart Healing Training. As Elise Tarango taught how to conduct a heart healing session where we invite the Savior to be present with us as we clear blockages to abundance and healing, she explained that we must "dive in through the door of appreciation and gratitude."[52] As she spoke, the Spirit bore witness to me that her words applied to prayer as well.

She explained how Dr. Karl Lehman, a psychiatrist, and Dr. E. James Wilder, PhD, discovered that the most effective way to start a conversation with God is through appreciation. Feeling and focusing on appreciation and gratitude in our bodies activates the ventral vagal nerve, which is responsible for our safe, social, connecting state. Activation of this nerve turns on circuits in our brain referred to as relational circuits. These relational circuits help us feel safe enough to bond, feel connected with others, and build relationships. So, when these relational circuits are on, our time spent with the Father can be a time of bonding and connection. Dr. Lehman teaches, "When we are in a state of [relational circuits] being ON, we are seeing God and/or others as a presence/person to love and be loved, to know and be known, to empower and be empowered."[53] This is the space we hold as we experience and feel true appreciation in our prayers.

Melissa Romano is a holistic therapist that specializes in the human ability to connect and communicate with others. She also focuses on healing approaches based on our body's movement, breath, and sensations. She highlights relational circuits in her work and suggests that they can also be turned on through the "foundational trinity for connection."[54] This foundational trinity is grounding, orienting, and resourcing. And by doing these three things, we are naturally led to a state of gratitude, which turns on our relational circuits.

How can you ground, orient, and resource?

The first part of the foundational trinity is grounding. Romano's definition of grounding is to bring awareness to where your body touches the earth. Can you notice where your body touches the earth right now? Are your feet on the ground? Are you sitting on a chair that is supported by the ground? Are you snuggled on a couch that sits upon the earth? Feel the ground beneath you and how it supports your body. Where do you feel that right now?

The second part of the foundational trinity is orienting. Orienting is moving our awareness from the earth and ground to the literal space around us. It is becoming aware of your location in time and place. Look around. Where are you? Are you inside a house, which is inside a city, inside a state, and inside a country? Where are you on the timeline of the seasons? Is it spring? Fall? Summer? Winter? What is the time of day? Is it morning? Afternoon? Evening? Notice where you are in time and place.

The third part of the foundational trinity is resourcing, which is noticing the resources you have. For example, resources might be what your physical senses give you. What colors can you see as you look around? What emotions do you feel in your heart? What resources are in your home? Maybe a family picture nearby reminds you of your family—a resource of love and support. Maybe a tree out in the yard catches your eye, reminding you of the resource of life and beauty.

Perhaps a messy kitchen invites thoughts of the resources of food and nutrients you have access to.[55]

Grounding, orienting, and resourcing helps move you to a space of gratitude. Can you feel deep appreciation in your heart right now? Can you feel it pulsing in your body? If so, what might happen if you now approach Heavenly Father in prayer? What kind of conversation might you have with your relational circuits turned on due to the gratitude you are feeling?

Approaching God in appreciation is preparatory for a mighty prayer. On the other hand, when we approach God because of frustrations, anxieties, heartaches, or stress, our relational circuits are "off," and our ability to connect with the Father is stifled. In this state, "we see God and/or others as a tool to use, a problem to solve or a project to manage."[56] Approaching God as a tool to solve a problem does not nurture our relationship with Him. First, connect with Heavenly Father through the door of appreciation, and then express those difficult emotions to Him.

How else can you evoke deep, genuine appreciation?

Here's another way to access gratitude before praying: recall a time when you felt deep joy or appreciation—a walk on the beach, a time with family, a moment in the temple. This is not just about giving thanks. This is about recreating this moment in your body, your senses, and the space around you. Remember the details. Who was there with you? What did the sky look like? What were you wearing? How did you feel?

Then notice where Heavenly Father and Jesus Christ were during that experience. One of the Savior's many names is Emmanuel, which means "God with us."[57] So ponder on your experience and look where your Father and Brother would have been during this time. Finding Them in these moments deepens appreciation and shifts the space, or air, around you. Can you sense it? When I do this, I can almost feel the air around me become denser, thick with light and love and joy and appreciation.

The Apostle Paul wrote, "In every thing give thanks: for this is the will of God in Christ Jesus concerning you."[58] God the Father desires a connection with you. He loves you and wants to bond and commune. Take time to really sit in appreciation before having a conversation. I wonder how it might change your experience with prayer.

Again I bear witness that not one single, sincere prayer has been offered since the beginning of time that the Lord didn't respond to. Not one. Our problem is we don't ask.

—GENE R. COOK

The What Prayer

I still remember that rainy day, years ago when I was in high school. I had released-time seminary, and I was supposed to be in class. But I wasn't. I had been struggling with some teenage-high-school-thing that I'm sure was dire and life threatening at the time (as they always are). And I was in the bathroom crying.

I was angry, frustrated, discouraged, and sad. I remember spewing out all my feelings and thoughts to Heavenly Father, and, when I was done, I stopped. I waited. Nothing happened. So I asked this one question: "Why aren't You helping me?"

Very clearly, the thought came to my mind in a voice that wasn't my own. "Why don't you ask?"

At the time, I did not understand the power of this answer—or even what the words were telling me to do.

Fast forward to years later when I'm lying in my bed at night, troubled about how to parent a child exploring boundaries. I'm expressing my frustrations with Heavenly Father and saying things like, "Please help me to know what to do when she doesn't listen to me. Please help me to be a better mother. Please help me to respond in a way she needs." And in the middle of all of that, I was stopped. Once again, words came to me in a voice that wasn't my own. It said, "Ask: What do I do when she yells at me like that?"

I was stunned. I had never thought to ask such a specific question in a prayer before.

I was quick to take the advice this time, and I asked, "What do I do when she yells at me like that?" Suddenly, my mind was flooded with how to respond to my daughter when she yells at me.

I was shocked. I had never received such an immediate, detailed answer from a prayer before. But then again, I had never asked such a specific, open-ended question before either.

When Joseph Smith was searching to know which church he should attend, he pondered on open-ended questions that required answers. He said, "In the midst of this war of words and tumult of opinions, I often said to myself: What is to be done? Who of all these parties are right; or, are they all wrong together? If any one of them be right, which is it and how shall I know it?"[59]

Joseph asked open questions:

- What is to be done?
- Which party is right?
- Are they all wrong?
- If one of them is right, which is it, and how will I know?

These are the questions he was pondering on. And when he went to pray to the Lord for help in knowing which church was true, he did not say, "Please help me to know which church to go to." He asked a question that required an answer. He said, "I asked the Personages who stood above me in the light, *which of all the sects was right* (for at this time it had never entered into my heart that all were wrong)—and *which I should join.*"[60]

When we have a face-to-face conversation with someone and want to know something, do we say to them, "Honey, please help me to know what your schedule looks like this week"? Or do we say, "Honey, what is your schedule this week?" Do we say, "Jan, please help me know what book you recommended me to read"? Or do we say, "Jan, what book did you recommend to me the other day?" We ask open questions that elicit answers.

Paul from the New Testament exemplifies this principle as well. When he was known as Saul and persecuted the Saints, he had a vision and the Lord identified Himself. Once Paul knew who he was talking to, he asked a mighty question: "Lord, what wilt thou have me do?" Paul asked an open-ended question, and the Lord gave a clear, specific answer: "Arise, and go into the city, and it shall be told thee what thou must do."[61]

Just as Paul asked the Lord a specific question, we too can ask Heavenly Father specific questions. Asking open questions that require answers will often result in . . . answers!

When I began asking question in my prayers, I began receiving answers almost immediately! My friend Nancy Crawford had a similar experience. She shares her story:

> I had been itching for at least five years. How do I know the timing? In the summer of 2020, we celebrated our 50th wedding anniversary by purchasing new bicycles from REI and almost every day we would ride. Everything was shut down in Washington because of Covid-19, and our days were spent riding our bicycles and enjoying nature.
>
> My husband and I rode fourteen miles daily on the Centennial Trail. Once a week we rode the Trail of the Coeur d'Alene's—a different section each time.
>
> It was a great time for us, except for one problem! When we returned from our rides, I would have a rash on my back that itched terribly! It seemed like the cause was sweat. But it would appear when I wasn't sweating also, so that couldn't be it! Months later, I had allergy testing done but everything came back negative.
>
> I felt like I had nowhere to turn for help in the medical community, so I decided to ask God. I desperately wanted to know, and I prayed daily, asking specifically, "What is making me itch?"
>
> I pondered my question constantly.
>
> One day while pondering, these words came to my mind: "It is your wedge pillow." Grateful for an answer, I washed the polyester cover, put it on the foam pillow, then covered it with a thick fleece blanket so I would not come in contact with the polyester. But that was not the end of the itching. It was better, but I felt there was something else. I continued to pray and ponder, and again some words entered into my mind, that were not my thoughts: "It's the nuts."
>
> I stopped eating nuts. The itching stopped.

Interestingly, while I was itching all these years, my white blood count (WBC) had been in the "Low" range since 2021. Recently, I was referred to a hematologist and she wanted me to have more lab work done. Through the spirit, I came to an understanding that my low blood count was because I had an allergy to nuts and I stopped eating them five days before I had the blood work done. I was confident that my WBC would be higher—It was almost normal!

Pleased, my doctor said that we needed to test it again in January 2025 and she would meet with me on February 5th. I continued to abstain from all tree nuts and had the blood drawn as requested. This time it was in a normal range. My doctor told me that my count was the highest one of the day and that she didn't need to see me anymore!

One might ask, why did I receive an answer that it was my pillow cover? I think it was, partially, but not the full answer. Also, perhaps, I was being tested to see what I would do to act upon what I had been given. When I acted in faith, I received more.

I know that we can receive answers to our prayers! This is just one example of how I have been blessed.[62]

What questions can you ask in your prayers? What do you need to know in your life right now? What specific guidance are you searching for? How can you ask questions to get those answers? Here are some ideas:

- What can I do today to improve my relationship with my spouse?
- What can I eat right now that would be good for my body?
- What do I need to do when _____ happens?
- What can I say when _____ happens?
- What verse in this chapter of scripture specifically applies to me today?
- What questions can I ask as I listen to conference to receive the inspiration I need?
- What would I ask if I knew what to ask?

I even ask yes or no questions, and when I bring my awareness to my stomach and chest area, I can sense a difference in how I feel. "Yes" often feels like a lightness in my core. "No" feels heavy. What might "yes" or "no" feel like for you? You can ask, *right now*, what it feels like in your body. Pray to Heavenly Father and ask, "Heavenly Father, what does a 'yes' feel like in my body?" Then take some deep breaths and see how you feel. Now ask, "Heavenly Father, what does a 'no' feel like in my body?" Take some more deep breaths and see how you feel. The change will be subtle, and with practice, you will be able to identify it more easily.

One of my favorite open-ended questions is, Is there more? I ask this after I have received my initial answer or impression. I learned this from Elder Richard G. Scott when he shared about a time when he was attending a Sunday School class:

> In that environment, strong impressions began to flow to me again. I wrote them down. The message included specific counsel on how to become more effective as an instrument in the hands of the Lord. I received such an outpouring of impressions that were so personal that I felt it was not appropriate to record them in the midst of a Sunday School class. I sought a more private location, where I continued to write the feelings that flooded into my mind and heart as faithfully as possible. After each powerful impression was recorded, I pondered the feelings I had received to determine if I had accurately expressed them in writing. As a result, I made a few minor changes to what had been written. Then I studied their meaning and application in my own life.
>
> Subsequently I prayed, reviewing with the Lord what I thought I had been taught by the Spirit. When a feeling of peace came, I thanked Him for the guidance given. I was then impressed to ask, "Was there yet more to be given?" I received further impressions, and the process of writing down the impressions, pondering, and praying for confirmation was repeated. Again I was prompted to ask, "Is there more I should know?" And there was. When that

> last, most sacred experience was concluded, I had received some of the most precious, specific, personal direction one could hope to obtain in this life.[63]

Elder Scott's experience is similar to my own. And it can be your experience too. Whether you're asking open ended or yes/no questions, you are opening the door for communication with Heavenly Father. When we ask, He answers! And when He answers, we can ask if there is more.

When I find myself slipping into my old habit of "please help me" pleadings, I stop myself and say the word *what*. Starting that question helps me to be present and ponder what I really want to know. In this moment, my heart is allowed to influence my mind, and the words flow for the questions I need to ask.

Asking "what" questions in prayer not only elicits answers from the Divine, but it can also shift our perspective. It allows us to see more clearly our own responsibility for our lives. For example, rather than saying, "Please bless . . ." and then waiting for that to come about, asking, "What can I do when this happens?" accepts the power of agency. It communicates with Heavenly Father in a way that implies, "I understand the power I have with my agency, and I desire to use it. I accept responsibility for the way I use this power. Please lead me in it." Nancy is a great example of this. Instead of asking, "Please help my itchy skin to stop," she asked what the cause was and then used her agency to act on the promptings.

Allie Duzett talks about imagining a person on their knees, praying and praying.

> And they're very upset because they've been praying the same thing over and over and really, *really* wanting answers. They want to be saved. They want all their problems to go away. They want to stop feeling the way they feel. And they totally mean it. They are so sincere. But they feel like it's not being heard because that prayer cannot be answered.[64]

What? The prayer cannot be answered? Is that true?

She goes on to explain, "The prayer they are praying cannot be answered because they are not willing to accept the full truth of how the universe works. They want these changes to happen while continuing to deny the role of agency in life."

Might our prayers be unanswered because what we are praying for involves someone else's agency? The heartfelt pleading of "please bless my wife to stop being narcissistic" involves agency. What might happen if we ask, "What can I do to feel loved even when my wife is narcissistic?" How might our experience of life change if we focus more on the power of our own agency and how to use it? Asking "what" questions in our prayers acknowledges ownership of our agency in the things we need or desire that align with God.

Before I learned to ask specific questions, my prayers were full of "please help me feel the Spirit more," "please help me to do well on the test," "please bless the food," "please help me to get a scholarship." As I look back over my life, these prayers were answered, sometimes in ways that I didn't expect or didn't see.

However, when I pray and ask specific questions, I don't need a lifetime to look back and see the answers. If I am in a state of listening and feeling, I am answered often immediately.

I am excited for the experiences that await you when you ask open-ended questions in your prayers. I wonder what answers you will receive.

You go to the Lord regardless of the condition of your soul, and He will respond. He never closes the door against you.

—TRUMAN G. MADSEN

The Eternal Gratitude Prayer

Alma the Younger teaches us about the relativity of time when he says, "All is as one day with God, and time only is measured unto men."[65] If "all is as one day with God," that means our past, present, and future are all in one: right now, in this moment, we are living in the past, the present, and the future. This is an eternal perspective.

The Doctrine and Covenants expresses a similar concept describing where angels reside: "They reside in the presence of God, on a globe like a sea of glass and fire, where all things for their glory are manifest, *past, present, and future, and are continually before the Lord.*"[66] We can practice having the past, present, and future before us as we pray.

This is a tall task for the human mind. How can we do it? One way I have found is to imagine myself after I have been resurrected, perhaps beyond the Millennium and Judgment Day. And even at a time after that when all has been reconciled by the Savior. Can you imagine that time? I believe at that time, with all reconciled, that most likely the problems I am facing right now will be resolved. Hooray! That will be a glorious day. With this in mind, I give thanks today for the resolution of my problems and trials I am currently in the midst of.

Right now, we are a family of nine. Our oldest is sixteen, and our youngest is three. Our home is wonderful, but we are pushing its limits to house all of us. Without an eternal perspective, I could pray for a larger house, money for adding on, or anything like that. But with an eternal perspective, I know we will have made it through (though, I'm not sure how!). In the end, we'll have survived these challenging family-growing years. So this is what I can give thanks for in this moment. I can tell Heavenly Father, "Thank you for helping us get through small spaces with our large family."

I've said prayers like, "Thanks for helping my daughter's congestion get better," amidst her sniffling and sneezing. And, "Thanks for helping my little son sleep through the night," even mornings after he was up out of his bed at midnight and then tossing and turning in mine. With an eternal perspective, *someday* he will sleep through the night, and *someday* her perpetual stuffy nose will breathe freely, so I can give thanks for the future right now in the present.

Elder Bednar shares about a time when his wife was invited to pray solely giving thanks. Even though he doesn't say if she approached the prayer with an eternal perspective, he does say that she gave thanks for eternal things—that the Holy Ghost could bring comfort and that families can be together forever:

> During our service at Brigham Young University–Idaho, Sister Bednar and I frequently hosted General Authorities in our home. Our family learned an important lesson about meaningful prayer as we knelt to pray one evening with a member of the Quorum of the Twelve Apostles.
>
> Earlier in the day Sister Bednar and I had been informed about the unexpected death of a dear friend, and our immediate desire was to pray for the surviving spouse and children. As I invited my wife to offer the prayer, the member of the Twelve, unaware of the tragedy, graciously suggested that in the prayer Sister Bednar express only appreciation for blessings received and ask for nothing. His counsel was similar to Alma's instruction to the members of the ancient Church "to pray without ceasing, and to give thanks in all things" (Mosiah 26:39). Given the unexpected tragedy, requesting blessings for our friends initially seemed to us more urgent than expressing thanks.
>
> Sister Bednar responded in faith to the direction she received. She thanked Heavenly Father for meaningful and memorable experiences with this dear friend. She communicated sincere gratitude for the Holy Ghost as the Comforter and for the gifts of the Spirit that enable us to face adversity and to serve others. Most importantly, she expressed appreciation for the plan of salvation, for the

> atoning sacrifice of Jesus Christ, for His Resurrection, and for the ordinances and covenants of the restored gospel which make it possible for families to be together forever.
>
> Our family learned from that experience a great lesson about the power of thankfulness in meaningful prayer. Because of and through that prayer, our family was blessed with inspiration about a number of issues that were pressing upon our minds and stirring in our hearts. We learned that our gratefulness for the plan of happiness and for the Savior's mission of salvation provided needed reassurance and strengthened our confidence that all would be well with our dear friends. We also received insights concerning the things about which we should pray and appropriately ask in faith.[67]

As demonstrated in Sister Bednar's example, a tender miracle of an eternal prayer is that it can change the state within us. For example, I feel stressed when my daughter is constantly sick. Can I send her to school? Will they think it's COVID? *Is it* COVID? Is she sleeping well in the night if she can't breathe freely? All of these worries weigh me down. But when I give thanks for her healing and recovery, even in the midst of her sickness, I feel confidence and peace that it is in God's hand. I no longer feel stressed or worried. I am reminded God's got it!

Another example of this is if one of my children has strayed from the covenant path, this would cause me fear, stress, worry, and anxiety. I believe the scripture, "Train up a child in the way he should go: and when he is old, he will not depart from it,"[68] so right now I can thank Heavenly Father for their return. Instead of saying, "Please help my daughter or son to return to the way," I can say, "Thank you, Heavenly Father, for guiding my them back to the covenant path. I'm grateful for the things they learned along the way that has rooted their testimony more deeply in Thee." Saying a prayer like this helps me to "look to Christ in every thought."[69] It also helps me to "doubt not" because I am exerting faith into His watchful care, and helps me to "fear not" because the end of the story—their returning to the path—brings me peace.

You can shift your thinking into the future state by asking yourself, A million years from now, will the problem I am facing be resolved? What scriptures assure you of the outcome? If you believe the words of the prophets, then you can give thanks today, as if the resolution has already occurred in this very moment—for, in a way, it has.

What challenges are you experiencing right now? What might this challenge look like in a million years? Will your relationship with your sister be repaired? Will your son's heart soften and return to the covenant path? Have hope in these things, and thank Heavenly Father for that, right now.

Another approach to the Eternal Gratitude Prayer is to maintain an eternal perspective that good can come from all things in your life. Thanking Heavenly Father for blessings that you don't yet see can expand your perspective of the situation. Paul says, "For our light affliction, which is but for a moment, worketh for us a far more exceeding and eternal weight of glory."[70] Jessica Garner, the woman who walked the beach in the "Answers for Mighty Pray-ers" section, writes about this.

> I have a special prayer activity that, for me, relieves resistance to virtually any situation I have faced. I learned it from the book, *The Hiding Place*, where Betsie comments on 1 Thessalonians 5:18 which says, "Give thanks in all circumstances." She then points out it doesn't say, *in pleasant circumstances*. Wow!
>
> So, in prayer, I say, "Thank you _____," and I list all off the things that I specifically don't feel grateful for! I thank my Heavenly Father for all the situations in my life that are sad, frustrating, hard, irritating, aggravating, and overwhelming. Everything bad in my life.
>
> For me, two magical and subtle things happen. First, I sometimes, not always, can actually imagine how maybe that bad thing could actually be a good thing for me. Just maybe. Second—and this is my main intention—I feel my resistance to the situation dissipate, just a little bit. Sometimes a lot. I just feel empowered to be a little bit more okay with it. And that makes life feel a whole lot better.[71]

Paul portrays this concept when he describes disciples of Christ who are "sorrowful, yet always rejoicing; as poor, yet making many rich; as having nothing, and yet possessing all thing."[72] Are we disciples who are sorrowful in difficult times, yet still rejoicing and giving thanks with an eternal perspective? Can we feel poor, and yet rich with an eternal perspective? Is it possible to possess nothing, and yet all things, as we focus on the past, present, and future? What hard things in your life can you exercise an eternal perspective on? What can you express gratitude for, that you don't feel grateful for yet? How might your perspective change if you try this?

Make prayer a constant and vital part of your life. Your spirit can come to depend on the sustenance and strength it receives from the Lord through prayer just as much as your physical body depends on the sustenance and strength it derives from food.

—VAUGHN J. FEATHERSTONE

The Image Prayer

In an online course titled The Science of Medical Intuition, instructor Norm Shealy, a neurosurgeon, said, "We do not have to pray, or think, in words. In fact, we do better by thinking in images."[73] He theorizes that all thinking ultimately occurs in images. For example, the word *hand* in English and *hand* in French are two different words, but they both bring to mind an image of a hand. "All words are just symbols that come out of our mouths for images," he stated. "Every thought is a prayer. We set in motion spiritual forces by our thinking, which is primarily in images."[74]

Have you ever prayed without words? The concept of praying with images—and the outcome—is beautifully described by Angie Asplund. She shares the following about her experience:

> By nature, I tend to visualize or see pictures of situations flash through my mind often. When my child is participating in an activity that I see as a potential accident waiting to happen, I will see them hurt and I feel that it has already happened. Whether it's a flash of a car accident, a visual of my kids arguing, or an illness getting worse, I can always see the worst that can happen in my mind.
>
> I'm sure we've all prayed prayers of fear where we see that terrible ending and then beg for that to NOT happen. Those kinds of prayers typically leave me feeling fearful of what's to come. The bit of hope in my words stays paired with worst case scenario pictures in my mind.
>
> In my quest for learning faith and my very active natural ability to see pictures in my mind, I decided to do something different. It felt radically different to me at

> the time. I started praying without words. And I replaced words with only pictures. I saw my child arriving to their destination safely, I saw my kids laughing together, I saw illness leaving the sick person's body. I instantly felt the different energy that this type of prayer left me with. I found myself smiling and feeling so full of faith and joy while visualizing these scenarios play out in my head. I ended these visual prayers with a hope in the future that was absent from my old prayers of fear.
>
> Not only did these visual prayers leave me feeling hopeful, but I started to see the results!! I saw my prayers were being answered. My visions were coming to pass, and I knew the reason.
>
> To begin a visual prayer, I invite you to see in your mind God the Father and Jesus Christ standing near you. Feel Their presence. Now see those pictures of what you want to happen. As you see the situations play out, feel how it would feel if it were happening. Now soak in the gratitude and joy of that beautiful blessing coming to pass. Stay in this feeling as long as you want. Feel free to explore visualizing what you are grateful for, visualizing angels helping you or those you love, visualizing your garden growing, your bank account overflowing or your light shining brighter. The possibilities are endless.
>
> When we see these visions in our head, we naturally feel the hope and faith that is needed to move the mountains in our lives. With that feeling, our words more easily match the energy of a hope and faith in what's to come.[75]

Moses, of the Pearl of Great Price, described his people's sad state by saying, "For their hearts have waxed hard, and their ears are dull of hearing, and their eyes cannot see afar off."[76] Can your eyes see afar off? Can you visualize your prayers? What would you like to see happening in the future?

Perhaps you would like to see a business venture become successful, or maybe you would like a sick loved one to gain health. Would you like a relationship to improve?

When we allow others their agency but we want the outcome to change, what power do we hold in us? Maybe you have a narcissistic father who deeply hurts you. Do you have to wait for him to change his behavior before you can feel love in his presence? Or could you pray an image prayer? If you allow him his agency, what could you imagine?

I would visualize something like this: The living room in your parents' home. There's the couch. The pictures on the wall. And there you are! You walk into the room and sit down. You feel nervous. Anxious. Unsure what it will be like when your dad walks in. And then, there he is. You see him enter.

In that moment, his childhood flashes before you—the trauma he endured, the pain and loneliness he suffered, the life he lived that has made him who he is now, even if he grew up in a good home.

He rattles off a snide, expected remark to you. Normally it would sting, but this time it doesn't. You see him as a small hurting child, and amidst his comment, you feel compassion for him. Your heart is full of love.

Were you able to see that? Were you able to watch yourself feel peace and love with your father? What might happen if you watch this every night before you go to sleep?

"He who hath faith to see shall see."[77] Do you have faith to see? What images can you imagine that you would like to see happening in your life? How might an Image Prayer bring you hope over fear?

It is in the relationship that healing arises.
Relationships, healing, and love arise together.

—BEN PAGE

The Five-Year Prayer

Just as it takes time to play a game of chess and intentionally place every piece to win, blessings often take time to materialize. Some blessings require a move to a certain location, or attending a certain ward so you meet specific people with spiritual gifts to bless you. Some require waiting for the new CEO who will see your hard work and promote you. This can be the case in every area of your life—school, hobbies, community. People and situations are placed in divine alignment. But all of that takes time. So, pray for that alignment now!

This idea of praying in advance comes from Allie Duzett, who encourages thinking ahead to the future and then setting the wheels in motion by praying for the future now. She encourages listeners to start asking the Divine for guidance and blessings now on situations that have not yet occurred. Duzett says,

> I started praying for my children's protection against child abuse basically before my kids were born. This is the time to be praying now for your grandchildren to be protected. This is the time to be praying for blessings on your next house. To make sure your next furnace doesn't go out. You know, we [need to] think ahead. We start praying now for our future car, for when our kids go to college, for when they have children of their own, for their future spouses. We start praying now for the stuff that hasn't happened yet—and won't happen for a long time. Now is the time we are going to set those wheels in motion.[78]

We can pray now for our future selves. We can pray for our health to improve so when we get sick, our body is better prepared to fight it. We can pray for a bright mind and the ability to be present with those we love during the last years of our lives. We can pray to forgive future offenses swiftly and completely, recognize future promptings and guidance clearly, and face our future trials with immovable faith. What future trial might you bless yourself with by praying for yourself now?

We can pray for our children's futures, too. Even though my oldest daughter is finishing her third year of high school, I have already begun praying that her college experience is full of positive, uplifting moments, that she will find encouraging and supportive friends, and that she will manage her challenges by turning to the Lord and strengthening her testimony. I also pray for my second daughter who recently underwent a spinal fusion to align her scoliosis. Even though she's only starting eighth grade this year, I pray now that she will find physical activities in high school that are enjoyable and will strengthen her body. I pray that she will discover strength within herself, in her voice, and in her worth. And I pray that she can be a light and lead others, rather than be led by them.

What might your prayers look like if you applied this concept to President Gordon B. Hinckley's encouragement:

> Fathers and mothers, pray over your children. Pray that they may be shielded from the evils of the world. Pray that they may grow in faith and knowledge. Pray that they may be directed toward lives that will be profitable and good. Husbands, pray for your wives. Express unto the Lord your gratitude for them and plead with Him in their behalf. Wives, pray for your husbands. Many of them walk a very difficult road with countless problems and great perplexities. Plead with the Almighty that they may be guided, blessed, protected, inspired in their righteous endeavors.[79]

We can pray for our grandchildren (and great-grandchildren and great, great-grandchildren!) to have opportunities to share their testimonies with their friends. We can pray for positive bonding future family reunions or girls camps or even Easter Sundays. We can even combine this prayer with a "what" prayer and ask, "What can I do now to prepare my spirit for the future?"

Consider the blessings you may need in five, ten, twenty, or thirty years. What blessings might your spouse, children, friends, siblings, parents, and even the sisters and brothers you minister to, need in five years? Begin praying for these blessings now.

Another angle of praying for the future is to pray for future wisdom without the difficult trials that usually come before. Duzett talks about requesting from the Lord understanding and knowledge prior to—or even without—difficult trials:

> When I was a child . . . I realized I needed to start praying to learn my lessons ahead of time without the trauma. [I] felt like if the point of life was to teach us a lesson—you know, if we're here to "learn our lessons,"—then could I please learn my lessons without the trauma? Could I please learn them from really good scripture study instead of from my dog dying or something? And so that is what I started praying for when I was maybe 12 or something. I would just pray, "Okay, God, teach me my lessons through study, instead of trauma." I didn't put it that way, but, you know, the 12–year-old version of that is what I prayed.[80]

What insights and understanding might you gain by praying this way? What heartache might be spared if you ask to gain wisdom through temple visits and scripture study and mighty prayers rather than through hardship and trials? How might your life be different? I don't believe all trials will be removed if we pray this way, but maybe there are a few that might be alleviated if we approach God with this intent.

The Psalmist wrote, "O send out thy light and thy truth: let them lead me; let them bring me unto thy holy hill, and to thy tabernacles."[81] This writer prayed for light and truth to come and lead him or her. The speaker asked to be blessed in the future. We can do this too.

I am now two years into using the Five-Year prayer. As I look back, I see how Heavenly Father has responded. He is generous and kind. He is the Great Responder. I wonder how He might respond to you—simply because you preemptively pray for yourself and others.

Duzett says, "I feel like my own prayers from my past self have been answered, and I also feel like because I do this, I'm blessing my future self every day."[82] How can you bless your future self? What blessings of abundance can you ponder on and request now? What can you pray for that you will need in five years?

It has been said, "prayer is made up of heart throbs and the righteous yearnings of the soul."

—JAMES E. TALMAGE

The Pulse Prayer

In May of 2023 I traveled to Yorkshire, England, to complete my training to become a certified forest therapy guide. We spent the whole week outdoors in beautiful weather on beautiful land amongst beautiful people. Our group was small—about ten participants—but just by wandering in a forest for an hour or two and then coming together and sharing the experience with each other, I felt a deep sense of peace, love, and unity.

During the day, I walked the green rolling fields of Broughton Sanctuary. I'd wander past the bleating sheep or into the grove of trees to sit in their shade and admire their surface root tapestry. I'd hear the cuckoo bird call, and I'd marvel at the tiny yellow buttercup flowers that triggered childhood memories I hadn't thought of in decades. In the evening, I would gather with my group around one large table and have a family-style meal of roasted butternut squash soup with fresh rosemary and sage or coconut quinoa curry with sweet potatoes, purple cabbage, and cilantro. We shared stories of our lives and our love for nature.

The night before the training was over, I pondered on how to bring all of this feeling, these sensations of calm and unity, home with me. I focused intently on the this, and I soon noticed I could feel a pulsing feeling in my heart area. I could feel the space around my heart, the space in my heart, the life energy that composed it, and the beating of it. I thought of the Psalmist, who said, "Commune with your own heart upon your bed, and be still."[83] I pondered how I could actually commune with my literal heart and not just my head during my prayer.

An idea came to me—to pulse a prayer from my heart—to send a prayer with images from my mind and feelings from my heart, without using any words. If I could do this, maybe this could be a way to practice including my heart in prayer.

I decided to try it.

I thought of the happy moments my group had shared together over the past few days. I was so grateful for these. I gathered them all together in my mind, felt that love and happiness in my heart, and then without words, felt my heart push a wave of that outward to heaven. It was as if I had gathered my sweet memories into an energy ball, placed that in my heart with all the joy and love that were associated with them, and then pushed that ball to heaven with joy and gratitude. I thought my heart would burst with warm feeling. It was amazing!

I decided to try it again.

Next, I tuned into what I was feeling—a bit of sadness when thinking about leaving this peaceful place and returning to a bit of chaos: a home with little children, more responsibilities, and a busy, bustling world. I was uncertain how I could bring with me the peace I was feeling now. I gathered those wonderings and concerns together, the images of me here and me there, and the confusion and sadness I was feeling. I bundled them all up and pulsed them out.

I watched as this pulse prayer—it looked like a blast wave!—moved out of me toward the horizon. In my soul, I knew it was heading to Heavenly Father. And I knew He was receiving it.

Throughout the last bit of my time in England, I pulsed prayers often. It was as if I was exercising my heart muscles, teaching them to do more than they had ever done before. And I know Heavenly Father received every one of those prayers. He appreciated the gratitude I sent Him, and He helped me integrate the calm I experienced in England to here and now. I love doing the Pulse Prayer!

Here's how you can do the Pulse Prayer:

Scan the past few days. What has been on your mind and heart? A difficult and strained relationship? Some quiet, beautiful time with a loved one? A success you have desired for a while? What is coming to your mind?

What emotions have been hanging around you lately? Delight in spending time with a loved one? Worries for a child? Anger toward a disrupted relationship? What have you been feeling? Sometimes just getting the hard feelings out of you can help you feel better—and sending them to God is a great way to get them out of you.

Pick one of these things you'd like to pulse out in prayer. Gather it all up and put it in your heart, whether it be thoughts or images or memories or feelings. Imagine they are contained in a bubble. Visualize your heart area with this bubble, and allow your body to feel all the emotions surrounding it. These emotions won't control you. It's okay to feel them in your body.

When you're ready, take a deep breath and explosively push the bubble containing emotions from your heart. Watch it spread out across the land into the horizon and know that Heavenly Father has received it.

Practice this often, any time you recognize intense emotions—whether positive or negative. Let this be a form of prayer for your soul.

I wonder what kinds of experiences you will have as you do this.

Our greatest misery is really not want and pain,
but distance from God.

—UNKNOWN

The Because Prayer

My family and I were fortunate enough to discover David Bowman and his "Drawn In" Come Follow Me videos at the beginning of the COVID pandemic. He has a fun, instructional way of explaining the scriptures and teaching young children (and old!) to recognize gospel principles. My favorite part in these videos is his discussion on how to apply the principles in our everyday lives. In one episode, he taught us how to pray the Because Prayer.[84]

Many times, we fall into the habitual use of specific phrases while praying. "We're thankful for this day," "Please help us to travel home safely," and "We're thankful for this food." Bowman encourages the use of "because" after each of those phrases. For example, we could say, "We're thankful for this day *because* we get to eat dinner together as a family." We could also say, "Please help us travel home safely *because* we love each other and we don't want anyone to get hurt. We want to spend the rest of the day together." Another idea is to say "We're thankful for this food *because* it fuels our bodies, and we need our bodies to go to the band concert tonight."

Some of the reasons you come up with might sound ridiculous, but they might actually be truth. I *am* grateful for food to fuel my body because I *do* need to go to my daughter's band concert tonight. It requires us as the pray-er to stop, be mindful and present, and dig a little deeper into the heart and mind of why we are saying what we are saying. Sometimes we might even surprise ourselves with what comes to mind. "Please help my daughter to make better choices today because . . . I feel like a bad parent if she doesn't." When this happens, I believe Heavenly Father is allowing us to recognize a limiting belief we are harboring. This is a great opportunity to take this belief to Him for healing, or to do the visualization described at the beginning of this book.

Saying "because" in prayers has become a new habit in our home. Every night, even my littlest ones pray this way. I hear things like, "We're thankful for this day because the missionaries came over and shared about their mission with us," or "We're thankful for this day because we got to watch a movie." I love to hear my children pray this way—it lets me see into their hearts more deeply. I believe Heavenly Father feels the same way. Even though He knows our hearts already, He is delighted to hear what we have to say to Him.

Once again, Jesus Christ is the great exemplar in this prayer. Let's return to the moments before raising Lazarus from the dead. The Savior said, "Father, I thank thee that thou hast heard me."[85] We can easily replace "that" with its equivalent "because" in this phrase: "I thank thee *because* thou hast heard me." The Savior was specific in His thanks and told the Lord why he was grateful. We can too.

Try it! After every phrase in your prayer, follow it with "because."

- Why are you thankful for this day?
- Why are you asking that you can sleep well?
- Why are you asking to travel safely?
- Why are grateful for your food?

The answers might seem obvious, but to question your mind and heart this way, to acknowledge the underlying reasons and put those reasons into words, you strive for deeper communion with Heavenly Father. It encourages you to be present and mindful. And He will be delighted with it. Those are the mighty conversations that foster relationship with Him.

The Music Prayer

Sister Thornock was an elderly neighbor down the street from us. She made amazing fudge and was also the director of our piddly small-town ward choir. I think I had a special place in her heart because each Sunday when she smiled at me, I would feel like I was making her day.

One Sunday when I was a teenager, the bishop called me to be the choir pianist. My mom was my piano teacher, so I had started lessons at a young age and felt somewhat confident to magnify this calling. I committed to it.

I was the choir pianist for about three of my high school years. Every year on Christmas, we sang the same song: "Birthday Party for the King." After a while, I think the congregation knew the words by heart and eventually joined in.

One other song I remember playing with the choir was "The Lord's Prayer." It was a bit challenging on the piano, but our small-town choir with their dedicated Sunday practices and a few off-key pitches made it sound okay.

I didn't think about this song for many years, but it recently popped up on our Sunday play list. It was the famous Andrea Bocelli and Mormon Tabernacle Choir version (now known as The Tabernacle Choir at Temple Square), so it sounded a little better than our ward's performance. As I listened to it, the sounds of the song entered my heart.

Our Father which art in heaven,
Hallowed be thy name.[86]

I could sing the words in my mind with the choir and Bocelli; I knew them by heart from all those Sunday practices years ago. And as the voice in my mind mixed with the music playing, I felt the air around me soften into stillness. I felt my heart expanding and offering honor to my Heavenly Father. I felt this movement into a prayer.

Thy kingdom come.
Thy will be done in earth, as it is in heaven.

I've never been one to quote a rosary. But for the first time, I understood how reciting the words of our Savior's prayer could create a heartfelt, genuine experience. I felt myself in complete alignment with this pleading. *Please, let Thy kingdom come. We are waiting. We are preparing. We are wanting.*

Give us this day our daily bread. And forgive
us our debts, as we forgive our debtors.

I found myself naturally scanning the past few days, discovering moments I needed to forgive others so I could be forgiven myself. As I sang along with Bocelli and the choir, I felt this song become a sacred prayer for me, asking for forgiveness of my own sins.

And lead us not into temptation,
but deliver us from evil:

Have you ever heard this version of the song? Take a moment to move away from distractions and look it up now—"Andrea Bocelli 'The Lord's Prayer' with the Mormon Tabernacle Choir." Before listening, take a few deep breaths. Better yet, let's set the mood. Go get in your car. Connect your Bluetooth and pull the song up on YouTube. Then turn up the volume and immerse yourself in the song of a prayer.

For thine is the kingdom, and the power,
and the glory, for ever. Amen"

Where does the music and words take your mind? What does that feel like in your body? What do you feel in your heart? Melancholy? Sadness? Peace? Joy? Sorrow? What does the air in the car feel like? Does it feel thicker? Thinner? Lighter? Heavier?

Listen to it again. Close your eyes. What do you see in your mind's eye? Moments of you with a newborn baby? Memories with a sister or brother? Or listen with your eyes open and look around. What do you see? If you are parked outside, do you see the beauty of the trees blowing in the breeze? The clouds floating by? God's majestic creations?

Did this song become a prayer for you? If not, how can you make it a prayer? What can you do to shift into a space of prayer as you listen to it?

Sister Thornock knew our songs could become prayers. I think she tried teaching us this in her own way, waving her arms excitedly, cuing voices and harmonies. She led us in this sacred moment of the Lord's prayer. I didn't quite experience it back then like I did yesterday, and I do now, as I listen to it and write this. But she knew. And God heard us. He heard our hearts perform this song, and He hears our hearts align with it now, in our cars, or our kitchens, or our offices, or our bedrooms. Wherever you might be.

How is a song a prayer for you?

What songs have become prayers for you?

In 2021, we discovered my then-twelve-year-old daughter had a large abnormal curve in her back. When she bent over, the right side of her back, ribcage, and muscles bulged upward. The X-ray revealed she had a sixty-degree S-curve in her spine. We moved into action—scheduled appointments with doctors, fitted her for a back brace, worked with chiropractors, attended structural-integration massage sessions, and visited Lowen Systems osteopathic practitioners. We fasted and prayed for a miracle that her body would respond positively to the work getting done on her. But at her follow-up visit, we learned that her curve had increased to seventy degrees. She would need a spinal fusion, joining rods and bolts into her spine to straighten the curve.

One day as I was driving, this trial was weighing heavily upon me. I was listening to a Christian radio station when I heard a song I'd never heard before. The lyrics pierced my heart. "I don't know how You make a way, but I know You will. . . . I don't know how You make a way, but I know You will."[87] Suddenly, I felt myself aligning with this statement, exerting energy into it, and believing it too. This moment of song and words became a prayer for me, expressing my faith to Heavenly Father that I truly did not know how He was going to make a way for my daughter, but I knew He would.

Have you ever experienced a song as a prayer? Have you ever listened to the rise and fall of the notes, the interweaving of the instruments and voices, and felt a message rise within you? If not, seek to hear a song in the next week that can be a prayer experience for you. God says, "For my soul delighteth in the song of the heart; yea, the song of the righteous is a prayer unto me, and it shall be answered with a blessing upon their heads."[88] What songs can become prayers for you?

When you cultivate a prayerful attitude, you embrace an ongoing spiritual connection as a way of life—a way of seeing through the eyes of love.

A prayerful attitude connects you to your sense of purpose and influence.

Connected to your higher power, you know that you never walk alone.

—ANGELA MONTANO

Mindful Prayers: Blessings on the Food

The idea to become a mighty pray-er over my food began when I first practiced mindful meditation. As I learned about the meditative practice, occasionally the discussion of "mindful eating" would surface. I began to be intentional about my thoughts before eating. The moments before I eat are usually spent in prayer, blessing the food, so this became a time of mindful prayer.

I truly delight in praying over my food now. There is a feeling of excitement and joy as I sit and pray. I enjoy it so much that sometimes I'll even take time to say a personal prayer after the blessing has already been said by someone else! I wonder if you will find as much joy in it as I do.

How can you pray mindfully and mightily over your food?

Look at the food before you. What are you eating? Is it a breakfast of scrambled eggs and toast? A bowl of oatmeal and raisins? Or cold cereal and fruit? Look at each item of food—each piece of it. Is there salt and pepper on the eggs? Jelly on your toast? Butter on your English muffin? Imagine where that item was before it got to your house. Was it on a shelf at the grocery store? Who put it there? Who was involved before it was shelved? Who got it to the store? And who was involved before it was received at the store? Who harvested it from the ground or gathered it from the hen? And before that, who planted or cared for it? How many hands helped prepare this food before you?

If you can imagine all those who helped provide your meal, then you can give thanks for them and ask that blessings be upon them. In your prayer, thank Heavenly Father for each one of these people. *For the hands that prepared this meal.* When I was younger, I thought that was in reference to my mother. But now, as I sit before my plate of food and imagine all these people, the "hands that prepared this meal" expands far beyond her. I am grateful for all these people who have contributed to this flavorful, nutritious meal.

You can also give thanks for the earth which grew the wheat for your bread, for the chicken who laid the eggs, and for the cow who gave its life for you. Taking note of all the resources and blessings of food available to you can also fill you with appreciation, turning on your relational circuits, and creating a sense of deep gratitude and connection with God. Extend this detailed gratitude for the grocery store shelf-stocker, the farmer, the harvester, the owner, and the truck driver, and request blessings upon them. Can you imagine all the blessings of love and joy these people could receive if everyone prayed for them with their relational circuits on?

After extending this gratitude to my Father, I ponder the needs of my body, mind, and spirit. I add to my mighty prayer what I would like the food to do for me specifically. I think about how it will go down my esophagus, into my stomach, get digested, and then be delivered throughout my body. Where do I need that food to go for the next twenty-four hours? To my sore back to heal? To my arms that will carry my baby today? To my brain for my test in geometry? You can ask for that specifically! If the quote on page 34 by Gene R. Cook is true—that every prayer is responded to—then think of the details you can ask for!

"Please let this waffle go to my legs this morning, for I will walk a lot (and maybe run!) through the airport for my business travels today."

"Please bless this lasagna to address the inflammation in my lower back to help relieve the pain."

"Bless this burger to direct its energy and nutrients to help my arm process the inflammation it is storing and repair the injury."

I even like to ask that the food help process my emotions.

"Father, please direct this food to my heart to heal the sadness it is carrying."

"I bless this sandwich to go to my brain and calm the anxiety I am feeling."

"Please bless this salad to help me process and release these unhealthy expectations I have toward my husband, and to help me direct my energy toward the Savior."

"Please bless this food with the power of the Atonement of Jesus Christ to assist my body to heal the areas I don't even know need healing." I have practiced this prayer for a few years now. Not over every blessing of food, but when there is an extra moment of silence before I eat, I take it. A small confirmation came to me just today—that this prayer was seen, heard, and responded to. I am a witness that He hears and responds to our heartfelt prayers.

I believe there is untapped power from our food that we can access just by asking for it in our prayers. Try it! Express detailed gratitude and then ask for what you need. Once you have done this, be intentional as you eat. Ask yourself, "What does this lasagna-with-God's-blessing taste like?" Can you experience the peppery basil or the creamy tomato sauce in a new way? Be present in the moment as you experience the many flavors and textures of your food that have new life in them from your prayer.

You can also combine the What Prayer with your mighty Mindful Blessing. What might come to you if you asked, "What can I do to make this food more nutritious for my body's specific needs?" Sometimes you might think to add a vegetable or a spice to the meal. Or sometimes, you might need to change your thinking about the food. I wonder what answers you get!

This reminds me of a story I read by Henri Rand Furgiuele, a Quantum-Touch practitioner. She wrote:

> [Twenty] years ago, I did an experiment with junk food that taught me a lot. At a time in my life when I was a strict vegan/raw foods person, I had great difficulty digesting anything that was not locally grown, organic produce.

One day, my guidance told me to drive through the fast food chain and order a burger, fries and milkshake. I resisted but finally did what that inner voice I trusted said to do. Sitting in the car, looking at that yucky food, I could feel stale oil going into the pores of my skin. Everything in me rebelled at having to put this into my body. Just the smell of it made me cringe. But I kept hearing in my head the word *consciousness*. So I tried to consider the consciousness of that food. I began to talk myself into seeing the vibrational consciousness *inside* this food. Underneath all the pesticides and chemical depletion, was there actually something that could be nourishing? I began to talk to the food, talk to myself, as if inside this food was actually a wonderful source-inspired vibration. The iceberg lettuce had been grown by loving hands. . . . It pulled in nutrients from the sun and all the elements. The buns came from fields of wheat saturated with nature's minerals. Gratitude to the animals, from whose body came the burger, filled me. On and on I went until I truly began to feel the vibrational presence that transcended the physical matter. I saw it, and felt it. In ten minutes, the meal transformed itself into a universal benevolence of light and well-being. Then as I ate, the vibration grew and grew. I felt oneness with all of reality, that the universe was supporting me in all possible ways, even in food that from the surface looked sadly lacking. The reframing so uplifted and elevated my whole being that I stayed that way for hours, even after eating, what on the surface, was complete junk. I have so many clients who are having difficulty with food . . . needing to control this or limit that or insert this or, or, or. . . . If they could see food not as just the biologic stuff of calories and food groups or how their body is shaped, but instead see/feel/sense the vibration of benevolence inside it . . . what a food truly offers, it just might help them rise above the material blocks.[89]

I wonder if that is one of the purposes of a blessing on the food. How can we nurture its light and energy as we mindfully pray before consuming? How can we use it in our body? How will it respond differently because of our request to Heavenly Father? Perhaps, the guidance from Heavenly Father to bless our food is because He knows of this power and wants us to have it. And finally, what rich flavors and textures can we intentionally notice to show honor and appreciation for God's gifts of life and nutrition to us? How might your experience change as you pray mightily over your food?

The Lord's Prayer

translated from Aramaic to English
by Neil Douglas-Klotz, PhD

O Birther! Father-Mother of the Cosmos,
you create all that moves in light.
Focus your light within us—make it useful:
as the rays of a beacon show the way.
Unite our "I can" to yours,
so that we walk as kings and queens with every creature.
Create in me a divine cooperation—
from many selves, one voice, one action.
Grant what we need each day in bread and insight.
Forgive our hidden past, the secret shames,
as we consistently forgive what others hide.
Deceived neither by the outer nor the inner—
free us to walk your path with joy.
From you is born all ruling will, the power and life to do,
the song that beautifies all from age to age it renews.
Amen.

Part III

The Nonviolent Communication Prayer

The final portion of this book is a discussion on the last mighty prayer I share with you. Whereas Part I introduced you to ideas about mighty pray-ers and answers to mighty prayers and Part II shared ways to pray with multiple senses, Part III discusses a powerful technique you can use that will help you encounter Heavenly Father in a new way.

The following portion might feel dense and thick, but internalizing the concepts and employing them in prayer will open doors for your prayer experiences. The following concepts were so life-changing to me that I include a few quiz questions, practice sentences, and even some graphics to help clarify the concepts.

The energy you expend in a genuine exploration of this prayer technique will be valuable. It will prepare your heart and mind for sacred experiences with your Eternal Father.

Thus our prayers allow us to express to God our needs, our challenges, our deepest feelings and desires, and to ask sincerely for his help.

—ROBERT L. MILLET

The Nonviolent Communication (NVC) Prayer: Introduction

As mentioned at the beginning of this book, in the year 2020, I read a book that changed the way I viewed communication with other people. It is called *Nonviolent Communication* by Marshall B. Rosenberg. In this book, Rosenberg describes *violent* communication as any way that results in hurting or harming someone through communication—judging, bullying, blaming, speaking without listening, criticizing, being defensive, and more. Therefore, *nonviolent* communication is just the opposite: communicating with love, empathy, and compassion.

Nonviolent Communication is designed to help the reader navigate challenging, emotionally charged conversations with compassion and understanding. It gives guidance on how to move beyond responding defensively to responding compassionately, thus getting to the root of difficult conversations.

Rosenberg suggests several steps to accomplish this kind of communication. That disastrous Sunday evening—the day our children (and myself!) fought and screamed and cried while we tried to celebrate Easter—while lying in bed, it occurred to me to apply these four steps in prayer. I discovered that doing so gives us the power to explore our inner workings and communicate them clearly with Heavenly Father. Oren Jay Sofer, author of *Say What You Mean*, commentates on Rosenberg's teachings: "The core of Rosenberg's Nonviolent Communication model—observe, feelings, needs, and requests—offers a powerful template to investigate our own experience, thoughts, and emotions and to determine the essential components we wish to communicate."[90] This is a powerful tool when having a mighty prayer.

It may seem simple, so you may be tempted to skim the next chapters. But I encourage you to read deeply. The discussion in each section addresses specific aspects to each step that can really enrich the experience of an NVC prayer.

My conclusion of NVC can be summed up into four steps (observe, feel, need, and request). Following these steps is how I prayed that Easter Sunday. This prayer was before any Pulse Prayer, and before any What Prayer, or Because Prayer, or any other mighty prayer I prayed. The following was my first mighty prayer that became a pivotal experience in connection with God.

I started by telling Him my observation that our day had not gone as I wanted. Though I knew He knew this already, I still told Him. I described how there had been a lot of arguments and fighting. Many family members cried, including me. I explained siblings were unkind and said hurtful things to each other, and because of all this, we didn't sit down and talk about the Savior and His Atonement in the Garden of Gethsemane. We didn't talk about the beauty of His resurrection after His crucifixion. We didn't have any moments where the Spirit was felt.

As I told Him this, I realized that emotions were naturally surfacing and with them came new thoughts. It wasn't just that I was upset about our Easter Sunday. There was more. I hungered for feelings of the Spirit. I wanted to *feel* more. I wanted to feel the Spirit on our Easter Sunday. I longed to feel the light of Christ as we celebrated His life. I wanted my children to feel it too. In this moment, these realizations led me to discover something deeper. I realized I wanted to feel His love more in my daily life. I needed to feel Heavenly Father, His Son, Jesus Christ, and the Holy Ghost in my life more. I told Heavenly Father that I believed the only way I could do this was through highly-focused, long scripture study and prayer. And if I lived an extreme, imbalanced life of highly focused spiritual feasting, my children would be neglected, my home would be forgotten, and we would all go hungry day after day.

As I talked with my Father about the challenge to meet my needs for increased feeling, awareness, and sensitivity to the Spirit, I remembered step two of Rosenberg's nonviolent communication model: feelings. I addressed the emotions I felt around the situation: frustration and irritation because when I tried to study scriptures or to ponder or commune, my children would interfere. They would invade the sacred space I was attempting to create.

I continued to step three and stated very plainly what I felt I needed in this situation. “I need to feel. I need to feel the spiritual highs more. I need to feel more.”

And finally, I concluded with the last step of the process and requested Heavenly Father to help me in this. “Would Thou be willing to help me feel more?”

Surprisingly, I felt a clear impression.

Would you be willing to do what I’ve prompted and asked you *to do?*

Suddenly, my mind recalled the impression I had received three years before to start taking a small amount of time each day to meditate. Understanding flooded my mind—taking time to meditate would help me to live more in my heart, rather than exist in my head. Living more from my heart would allow me to feel more. I knew I couldn’t feel in my head; I could only feel in my heart. That is where the Spirit resides, and I needed to practice existing there more.

I was shocked to receive such a clear impression. And I believe I received it because I had truly prepared my heart by following the steps in *Nonviolent Communication.* I had cleaned my thoughts from judgment, expressed the tender feelings in my heart with accountability, recognized the need underlying all of my discomfort, and then requested help in what I was experiencing.

Nonviolent Communication is invaluable in learning how to communicate in a Christ-like way with others. It is a great resource for communicating with charity with your family, friends, associates, coworkers, and anyone else in your life. In addition to blessing your relationships with others, it can magnify your relationship with your Heavenly Father. Using the four steps in prayer will bless you with experiences and knowledge the Father wants you to have. It is a way to be fully present in prayer, a way to strip back any walls or barriers in communicating with Him, a way to open you heart and truly feel His presence.

My synthesis of the NVC technique into four steps—and its application to prayer—flow as described in the following chapters, but here is the super-condensed version. Step 1: Make an observation, step 2: express your feelings, step 3: articulate your needs, and step 4: request help. To help me remember, I focus on one key word for each step: Observe. Feel. Need. Request.

The steps may seem simple—too simple. It may cross your mind that the prayer won't work. Don't give up on it. Continue reading. Take note of the tiny details that provide clarity on each step, and then try it out for yourself.

The intent of the NVC Prayer is to open *your heart.* It's allowing yourself to acknowledge your imperfections—be vulnerable and admit your weakness. You don't need to follow the steps outlined in the following chapters to do that, but having these guidelines helps me remember what to address and opens my mind to broader perspectives. It helps me stay clear of passing judgment, which blocks my heart from hearing Him. It helps me discover what's in my soul, guides me to pour it out to Him, and brings me closer to His wisdom and love.

The NVC Prayer can do this for you too.

The NVC Prayer in a Snapshot

After preparing for prayer by quieting your mind and heart, begin by explaining to Heavenly Father your **observations** of the situation. In this step, you are creating the setting. Once you have set the stage by vocalizing what you have observed occurring, express how the situation is making you **feel**. This step is where awareness of your inner environment is helpful. Now that you have expressed your emotions to your Father, progress to step three by stating the **need** you have regarding the situation. Do you need to feel more love? Do you need to be at peace? Do you need strength? And finally, in step four, humbly—without expectations—**request** help from God. Let's look at each step in more detail.

The Four Steps

Step 1: Observe

Imagine you are sitting on a park bench. You see a bird fly to the top of the maple tree across the way. You hear children playing and laughing on the playground. You smell the rotten food in the garbage can next to you. You watch a dog sniff the grass in front of you.

Now, considering the definition of *observe*—"to watch carefully the way something happens or the way someone does something, especially in order to learn more about it."[91] What did you *observe* about your imaginary day at the park?

Perhaps you observed the bird fly to the tree and saw the dog in the grass. You noticed the children playing and the trash bin next to you. And you might have observed the color of bench you sat on, or even the sway of the grass from the breeze.

What if you extend the observation to your other senses? What would you experience then?

You might hear the laughter of the children—and maybe some of their conversation. Maybe you hear the bird sing or the dog bark. Perhaps flies are buzzing around the trash can, or you hear the wind through the leaves of the maple. Do you feel a breeze on your forehead? And feel the sun resting on your skin? Or is it a cool, cloudy day?

All these mental images can be categorized as *observations*. Anything noticed through the five senses is an observation. What was seen? What was heard? Was anything tasted? Was anything touched or physically felt?

In step one, you observe the situation with your five senses and then describe it to Heavenly Father. Your job in this step is to simply use your five senses to tell Him what is going on.

For example, I might say something like, "My son tells me every day that he is bored. He has many toys and activities, but he does not play with them. Instead, he wanders around the house and tells me he has nothing to do." I am describing what I see and hear. This is a clear observation of how my son is acting.

Oren Jay Sofer says, "An *observation* is a concrete, specific, and neutral statement of an event, of what we see or hear in our environment, distinct from evaluation or interpretation."[92] When we state our observations in step one, we want to be careful not to evaluate, interpret, or judge. Evaluating, interpreting, or judging the situation imposes our opinions and standards on what is going on, which blocks our ability to expand our perspective and gain understanding. Disconnecting ourselves from opinions and judgments is powerful in a mighty prayer.

Making Judgments

Judging, the process of forming an opinion or evaluation by discerning and comparing, is something that we do daily. Let's consider what judgments we might make of the imaginary day at the park.

Perhaps there is snow falling and wind blustering outside your window. You think of your imaginary day compared to your current wintry day. "The day at the park was a beautiful day." Or maybe you are sitting at the beach, enjoying the crashing of the waves and the salty humid smell in the air. Comparing today to the day at the park, you think, "That day was awful—sitting next to a stinky garbage can."

The opportunities to judge are endless. But in essence, *forming an* ***opinion*** *or* ***evaluation*** *based on comparison is forming a judgment.* The moment we begin to judge, our hearts begin to close and we are not as open to connect with God, which defeats the purpose of the mighty prayer. There is a time and place for righteous judgment. But it is not now, in step one of an NVC prayer.

Rosenberg says, "We need to clearly observe what we are seeing, hearing, or touching that is affecting our sense of well-being, without mixing in any evaluation."[93] And Sofer says, "Applying careful attention, we tease apart the actual events—specific data in our environment—from the added layers of thought, perception, and reactivity."[94]

So, practice describing situations by simply using observations without evaluations. Use your five senses to help you steer clear from making judgments. "Verbs such as 'see' and 'hear' help us focus on the specific event rather than our interpretations."[95]

Helpful Hint: Use your five senses to observe.

Strictly observing and not judging can be hard. Sofer says, "It's natural to interpret and draw conclusions from our experience; it's part of how we navigate life. Our brains continually evaluate, discerning safety from danger, friend from foe."[96] Even from the time we are young, we are taught to evaluate, judge, and form opinions. In fact, my six-year-old in first grade just wrote her first opinion paper last spring: "Onions are the worst food. They are slimy. They are crunchy. They make people's eyes water. Onions are gross."[97]

If I had never tasted onions, I would probably agree—onions *are* the worst food. Yet, I have tasted them, and I love them. Might my daughter be missing out by forming this opinion and not trying onions? Might she learn to enjoy onions if she could remove the judgment, the blinder, that causes her to dislike them so much? We have yet to know . . .

Just like my daughter's opinion of onions has prevented her from being open to them, our own judgments blind us from being open, and, in this case, being receptive to what Heavenly Father wants us to hear and know. Our hearts must be open and free to communicate with heaven. We must check ourselves and strictly observe without judgment.

Let's look at the previous example of an observation: "My son tells me every day that he is bored. He has many toys and activities, but he does not play with them. Instead, he wanders around the house and tells me he has nothing to do." What would a judgment of this look like? Perhaps, something like, "My son is whiny." Here, I am forming a judgment of his character based on his actions. I am not describing what the scene looks like, nor am I using my five senses. I'm not making it visual for my Listener. I am only evaluating my son's behavior and character, judging him, or measuring him against some standard of whiny. I am measuring him on a spectrum with whiny on one end and content on the other, and then labeling him from that.

Helpful Hint: Placing someone or something on a spectrum, between two opposing things, is judging, *not* observing.

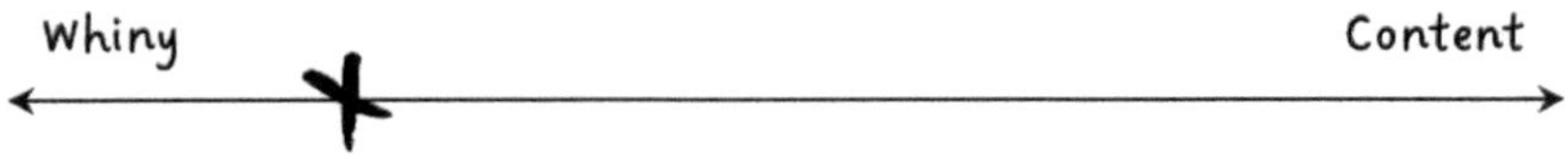

It is so easy to fall into the trap of observing a situation, then evaluating and labeling. Therefore, when we use labels, we are essentially saying that we have moved out of observation into judgment. Additional examples of labels might look like the following:

"My spouse is inconsiderate."

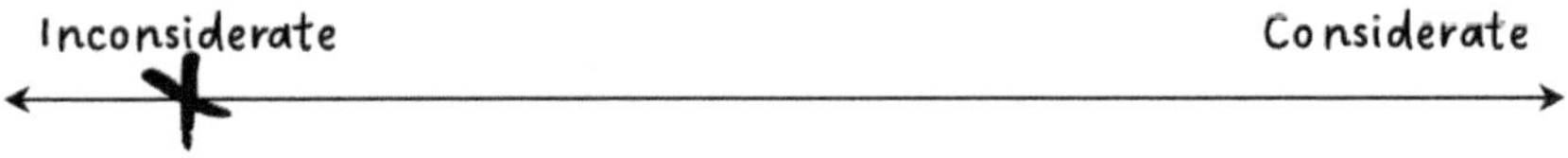

"My friend is so flaky."

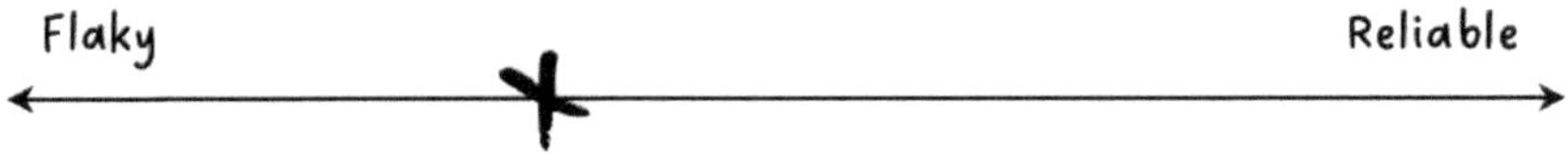

"My father is very critical of me."

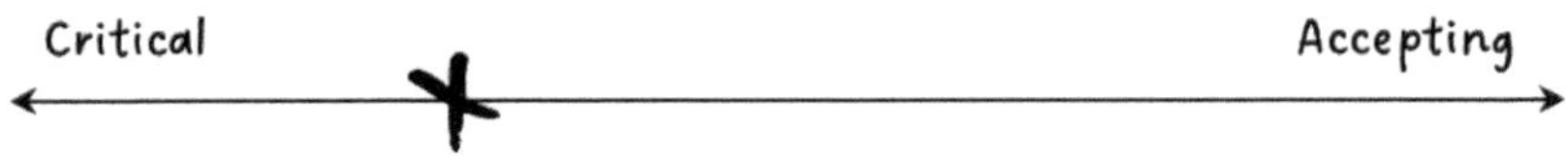

We might not consciously be labelling, but thinking of it it as a linear spectrum can help us recognize that we are evaluating and judging, not observing. With practice, we can begin to notice how often or seldom we place people, things, and experiences on a spectrum between perceived good or bad.

How might your life be different if you noticed this and consciously chose differently?

Helpful Hint: When you hear yourself saying "So-and-so is . . ." you are labeling, and thus, judging.

When this happens, take a step back and return to your five senses and continue on with your observation. All of your evaluations might be true, but they will not help you in your mighty prayer. When you are a Mighty Pray-er, you first approach God without any judgment. You only observe and then share that observation with Him.

Are the following examples judgment or observation?

Quiz 1

"Heavenly Father, my daughter chose to not attend church yesterday. When I asked her to get her dress on, she refused and remained in her room. When it was time for us to go, she wouldn't join us. She just yelled through the door, 'I'm not going today!' She also came home Friday evening from her friend's house smelling like alcohol."

What do you think? Were the five senses used to describe this situation? Was there any labeling?

In this example, the speaker described what she had observed about her daughter. This example of step one is free from judgment. It is a clear example of observation.

Quiz 2

"Heavenly Father, my daughter is so rebellious. We have taught her to obey the Word of Wisdom and to go to church, but we are pretty sure she drinks alcohol with her friends on the weekends, and when we ask her to get ready for church, she refuses."

What do you think of this one? Observation or judgment?

Were the five senses used? You could say the phrase "she refuses" is a summary of what was verbally said from the daughter's mouth. But what words did her daughter actually say? What exactly did the speaker hear from her daughter? What did she witness with her eyes? And what about labeling? "My daughter is so rebellious" is a labeling red flag. Here, the speaker has measured her daughter's actions, comparing them on a spectrum of what the speaker deems obedient versus disobedient. The mother has judged her daughter to be rebellious.

Take note to also watch for generalizations or exaggerations. We need to "avoid words that exaggerate or interpret: *always, never, ever, whenever, rarely.*"[98] These words are not concrete, specific, and neutral descriptors of the event, nor are they honest descriptions. If I told Heavenly Father that my son never listens to me, is that honest and true? Is it possible that maybe one time he did listen to me? I believe it is. Using the word *never* overlooks the time that he did, and is not an actual, true statement. It is dishonest to Heavenly Father and dishonest with myself. Being dishonest with Heavenly Father and myself does not put me in a position to receive clarity and truth from Him. Exaggerations and generalizations act as personal blinders to situations and will make it difficult for the heart to soften. If we are dishonest, even in the slightest, by using exaggerations, is our heart in the right place to receive His word?

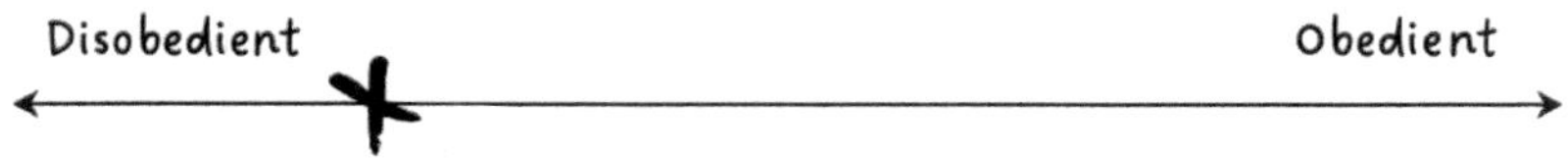

Helpful Hint: If you're using an exaggeration, you're stepping outside the boundaries of observation.

Sofer says:

> In training ourselves to make observations, we are cultivating a commitment to honesty. When we consider the difference between an observation and an evaluation, which is true? Is he really "being rude" or would it be more truthful to say that he did or said something that you didn't enjoy, that didn't meet your need for respect? Is it accurate to say that "[she's] never affectionate" or that "[she's] not as affectionate as I would like"?[99]

Approaching the Lord with an honest heart, void of exaggeration and judgment, is crucial for your mighty prayer. Begin as an observer—using your five senses without labeling or exaggerating—and then you are ready to move into step two.

Practice Sentences

Underline the statements that are observations.

1. My husband never does the dishes.
2. My kids left their toys out three nights in a row.
3. That driver swerved in front of me while I was driving.
4. Sara is so depressing to be around.
5. Joseph is lazy.
6. Peter always says he'll read his scriptures, but he never does.
7. Our money is low, and Blake's birthday is coming up.
8. He is ignoring me.
9. She walked past me while looking straight ahead.
10. You never answer my prayers.

Answers

1. My husband never does the dishes.

   Red flag! Did you catch the word *never*? Great job! I would not underline this sentence for it is using an exaggeration, and therefore not an observation.

2. <u>My kids left their toys out three nights in a row.</u>

   Can you "see" or imagine what's happening in this house? For three nights in a row, there are toys strewn all over. We don't know which toys, or where they were left, so this speaker could go into more detail. But this is a description, and thus, an observation.

3. <u>That driver swerved in front of me while I was driving.</u>

   I can visualize a vehicle swerving in front of someone. Can you? Again, it can be more descriptive, but the speaker used sight to describe what happened. If you underlined this one, good job!

4. Sara is so depressing to be around.

    Perhaps Sara is gloomy and weighing you down when you are with her, but what is Sara actually doing? I can't tell. Is she complaining about her job? Does she criticize you and other people? Does she gossip? I can't visualize the situation. Therefore, the labeling shifts the statement into a judgment, not an observation.

5. Joseph is lazy.

    Once again, this statement is in the judgment category, not the observation group. Joseph is being labeled as lazy. If you didn't underline this one, great catch!

6. Peter always says he'll read his scriptures, but he never does.

    Oh! Red flag! Did you catch the exaggerations? "Always" and "never." This statement is not an observation. I'd like to be able to visualize it. Does he say he will, and then he doesn't touch them? Or does he say he's reading them, and they're open in front of him, but he doesn't turn a page? What do his actions look like?

7. Our money is low, and Blake's birthday is coming up.

    None of the senses are used, but there are also no exaggerations or judgments. In this instance, I would reword the situation and give more details. As is, it leans toward being an observation just because it is a description of the speaker's state.

8. He is ignoring me.

    The speaker in this statement is looking at the man's actions and interpreting them as intentionally avoiding the speaker. The judgment of the man's actions is not an observation. Something like "he did not respond" or "he did not look at me" describes some of the five senses that had been observed—which would then be an observation.

9. She walked past me while looking straight ahead.

    This statement, on the other hand, is a visual description of a woman's behavior who could be judged as ignoring the speaker. But the judgment is left out, and we only see what the speaker saw. This is an observation. If you underlined it, way to go!

10. You never answer my prayers.

    Red flag! Did you catch it? "Never" is the exaggeration. This speaker gave their statement without any accurate descriptions of the situation. More description would lend to a more honest approach: "I prayed for help on my test, but I couldn't recall the words I had studied, and I got a C." Honesty and attention to detail create the foundation for the rest of your mighty prayer.

Practice making observations throughout your day—disconnected from judgment and free of exaggeration. This is an empowering way to shift your perspective of others and to prepare for mighty prayer.

Step 2: Feeling

The second step in the NVC Prayer is identifying and expressing your feelings. This is where you express how the situation is making you feel. Are you frustrated? Are you depressed and worn out? Are you brokenhearted and hopeless?

This might be a painful step to explore with Heavenly Father. This is where you allow those deep, difficult feelings to emerge so you can truly feel them, identify them, and express them.

I do this by quieting my inner environment and asking myself, "What am I feeling right now?"

Sometimes asking and allowing yourself to feel gives way for you to experience the intensity of your feelings. This can be scary! But sit with them and have compassion for yourself. These feelings will pass!

Sometimes our emotions might be present as physical pains in our bodies. Are your shoulders tight? What are you carrying there? Worry about your daughter? Anger toward your spouse? Is your gut tight? What are you storing there? Anxiety for a big work project? A son on a wayward path?

There are many resources online for words to help you name your emotions. The following is an incomplete list of words you can use to describe how you are feeling. It might be enlightening to select some of these words—even if you already know their meaning—and look them up in a dictionary. Reading the definitions will help to broaden your emotional vocabulary.

afraid	angry	annoyed	anxious
appalled	*bad*	bitter	blah
blue	bored	bugged	confused
crabby	cranky	critical	cross
crushed	dejected	depressed	destructive
detached	disappointed	disconnected	discouraged
disgusted	disturbed	doubtful	down
dread	embarrassed	empty	enraged
explosive	fearful	fed-up	fidgety
frightened	frustrated	fuming	furious
gloomy	grouchy	grumpy	heartbroken
helpless	hesitant	hopeless	horrified
hot	hurt	impatient	infuriated
insecure	irritated	let down	lonely
lost	low	mad	miserable
moody	nervous	offended	outraged
overwhelmed	panicky	regretful	repulsed
resentful	rotten	sad	sarcastic
sassy	scared	self-conscious	shy
stressed	tense	terrified	threatened
ticked off	timid	trembly	uncomfortable
uneasy	unhappy	unloved	vicious
violated	violent	withdrawn	worried

If you find yourself using the words *bad* or *stressed*, explore other words and see if you can come up with replacements. These two words are vague surface words that hide the true emotions you are feeling.

Rather than "feeling bad," are you feeling sad that you're not receiving attention from your spouse? Instead of feeling "stressed," are you feeling anxious that you have too many things to do?

Sit with your emotions and identify them.

Often, when I think I know how I'm feeling, I'll ask, "But what is under that? What is under the anger? Is it sadness? Fear? Embarrassment?" I keep asking until I feel I have found the root of it. This is a powerful exercise.

Once you know the root emotion, express clearly to your Heavenly Father how you are feeling. He understands and knows your heart and, as you open up to Him in this way, you will discover more about yourself.

Take a moment to look at the list of emotions again. Choose a few and say them out loud. How do they feel in your body? Do these words spark any thoughts? Bring anything to the surface? In the beginning, it might be helpful to use the list when you are at this stage in your prayer. Look over the list and see which ones you identify with in the moment that can guide you in expressing your feelings.

Helpful Hint:
Avoid expressing opinions and thoughts as feelings.

The above list is helpful because we often express *thoughts* instead of *feelings*, even when we use the word *feel*. Many of us have not been taught to recognize and identify our feelings, and we may think we are doing so, when we actually aren't. Rosenberg says, "A common confusion, generated by the English language, is our use of the word *feel* without actually expressing a feeling."[100] For example, you might say, "I feel like so-and-so doesn't care about me." This is not actually stating your emotional state but is an evaluation. Rosenberg gives three tips on how to notice if you're expressing a thought instead of a feeling.

1. Words that follow *feel*, such as *that*, *like*, and *as if* signal you are expressing a thought, not a feeling.

   "I feel *that* you should know better."
   "I feel *like* a failure."
   "I feel *as if* I'm living in a box with no escape."

2. Pronouns that follow *feel*, such as *I*, *you*, *he*, *she*, *they*, and *it* alert you that you are expressing a thought, not a feeling.

   "I feel *I* am constantly on call."
   "I feel *it* is useless."
   "I feel *he* just ignores me."

3. Names or nouns referring to people that follow the word *feel*.[101]

   "I feel *Amy* has been pretty irresponsible."
   "I feel *my boss* is being manipulative."

Ironically, when you are expressing a feeling, you don't need to use the word *feel*. Check this out: "I feel frustrated" versus "I am frustrated." Now, there is some debate about whether we should identify a feeling by using the linking verb. Some people say we shouldn't identify ourselves as emotions. But knowing you can say, "I am frustrated," to recognize it is a feeling can be a quick test to make sure you are expressing feelings, not thoughts. In the examples I share throughout this section, I will use *am* and *feel* interchangeably.

Helpful Hint:
Avoid labeling yourself when expressing your feelings.

Another mistake we often make when talking about our emotions is that we use *feel* to describe who we are. We might catch ourselves saying, "I feel inadequate as a mother." In this case, we are describing what we think we are, instead of how we are actually feeling. We are evaluating our ability to be a mother by meeting our ideal to keep the house clean and healthy food on the table, prevent our children from fighting, and assure they're praying daily. When we do this, we are actively judging ourselves.

Rather, we can express that we're disheartened, saddened, anxious, or exasperated. We can say, "I am downhearted that our house is cluttered. I can't stay on top of cleaning it." Or, "I am saddened that I do not meet the expectations my mother-in-law has for me."

Labeling ourselves, or describing ourselves, in explanation for how we are feeling is not our aim in this prayer. When judgment enters, our hearts are not truly open for revelation. Describe what you are feeling, not who you think you are.

In these examples—"*I feel sad* because I feel like I need to spend more time with my children and I am not," or "*I feel explosive* because I feel like I'm always make so many mistakes"—the speaker is not labeling but instead expressing their feelings, and then following it with reasons which are revealing and helpful for step three of the NVC prayer.

Helpful Hint:
Avoid judging your emotions as good or bad.

The Savior said, "Judge not."[102] Judge not others, judge not yourself, and judge not your emotions. Avoid labeling your emotions as good or bad. Don't measure whether or not they are appropriate. Don't shame yourself for feeling them. Just let them be! True healing cannot come if you don't allow your emotions to be recognized, acknowledged, and addressed.

Negative emotions are called "negative" not because they are bad but because they fall below the positive emotions on a scale measuring their vibrational frequency. Once again, if you are judging your emotions, then your heart is not open and ready to receive Heavenly Father's messages for you.

It is easy to shame yourself for having emotions. But, again, this will prevent clear communication between you and God. It is okay to feel the way you are feeling. Accept yourself where you are at. Allow yourself to be self-compassionate and present with your emotions. They won't last forever, and the healing that can come through the Atonement of Jesus Christ is powerful if you are able to allow yourself to be present with them for a time. I find myself experiencing this healing power every time I follow these four steps. You can experience this too as you allow yourself to be present with your emotions in step two.

Helpful Hint:
Accept responsibility for how you feel.

Finally, accept responsibility of your emotion. It might be easy to put the blame on someone else: "I am frustrated, because *she treats me so poorly,*" or "I am discouraged, because *he is not helpful around the house.*" But if you blame and focus on others, your heart is defensive and not ready to receive God's will. Rather, accepting responsibility of your emotions may sound something like this: "I am frustrated because I don't know how to respond when she speaks that way to me." Or, "I am discouraged because I want him to help more."

Rosenberg says, "What others say and do may be the *stimulus*, but never the *cause*, of our feelings."[103] He continues, "We accept responsibility for our feelings, rather than blame other people, by acknowledging our own needs, desires, expectations, values, or thoughts."[104] We accept responsibility for our own feelings by using the following phrase: "I feel . . . because I . . ." We might say, "*I feel* sad *because I* was really hoping she would come to church with us." Or, "*I feel* embarrassed *because I* want her to come to church with us."

If the speaker were not to accept responsibility, it might sound like this: "I feel sad because she didn't come to church with us." Or, "I feel embarrassed because she didn't go to church today." This blames the speaker's emotions on the daughter's actions. Can you feel the difference? Saying, "I feel sad because I was really hoping she would come to church with us" instead of "I feel sad because *she* didn't come to church with us" removes the blame from the daughter.

Accepting personal responsibility for your feelings is challenging. It can be a painful process, but it is worth it. Do the required soul-searching to discover what you are feeling and then accept responsibility for those feelings. This penetrating exploration allows emotions to be unearthed and prepared in order to be expressed to your Father in Heaven and given to your Savior, Jesus Christ.

Practice Sentences

Underline the statements that show accountability, and avoid blame, labels, and judgments.

1. I feel frustrated because my kids won't stop fighting all day.
2. I feel like I'm an embarrassment to my family.
3. I am stressed about my upcoming semester of school.
4. I feel lonely because I long for deep connection with others.
5. I feel disgusted with myself because I can't control my eating.
6. I feel like he is out to get me.
7. I am discouraged because I can't meet all my children's needs.
8. I am angry because he was unkind to me.
9. I feel I am always in trouble.
10. I am upset because I nag my husband all the time.

Answers

1. I feel frustrated because my kids won't stop fighting all day.

   This speaker blames the children for his or her feeling of frustration. When we are expressing an emotion, we want to accept responsibility for the way we are feeling.

2. I feel like I'm an embarrassment to my family.

   This statement uses the word *like*, and as Rosenberg suggests, this is an expression of a thought, or a judgment, rather than the speaker's feelings. I would not underline this.

3. I am stressed about my upcoming semester of school.

   This statement uses the surface word *stressed*, which doesn't explain a deeper emotion. I would not underline this and would instead search for other words to describe the feelings.

4. <u>I feel lonely because I long for deep connection with others.</u>

   This is a clear expression of the speaker's feelings. The statement contains the emotion followed by "because I," which shows the speaker accepting responsibility for the emotion, and includes an explanation for the cause of the feeling.

5. I feel disgusted with myself because I can't control my eating.

   Disgusted is identified as the emotion. Then the speaker takes accountability by concluding the root cause.

6. I feel like he is out to get me.

   The signal word *like* follows the word *feel*. I would not underline this as it expresses a thought—"he is out to get me"—rather than a feeling.

7. I am discouraged because I can't meet all my children's needs.

   This is similar to number five. It identifies an emotion (discouraged) and takes accountability by communicating the root cause.

8. I am angry because he was unkind to me.

   This is half and half. "I am angry" is an expression of an emotion, but "he was unkind to me" blames another. Here, to avoid blame we could say, "I am angry because I am hurt by the words that were said to me."

9. I feel I am always in trouble.

   This sentence is actually expressing a self-judgment. "I am always in trouble" is a generalization of yourself. Descriptions are not feelings, but judgment red flags.

10. I am upset because I nag my husband all the time.

    Yes! This is a clear statement for how this person is feeling and how they accept responsibility for those feelings.

Step 3: Need

After observing and then expressing, we are ready to address our needs. If we have stripped our observations and feelings from judgments and evaluations, then we are in a better place to discern the need at the root of the situation. Judgments mask the root of our need—what we really want to address with Heavenly Father. No wonder we are told not to judge!

By walking through the first two steps and then pondering on this third step, your awareness is heightened to the fact that "what others say and do may be the *stimulus*, but never the *cause* of our feelings."[105] This step helps us fully acknowledge the cause of our feelings—the need that is not being met. Rosenberg says, "We are accustomed to thinking about what's wrong with other people when our needs aren't being fulfilled." He continues, "Thus if we want coats to be hung up in the closet, we may characterize our children as lazy for leaving them on the couch. Or we may interpret our co-workers as irresponsible when they don't go about their tasks the way we would prefer them to."[106]

Did you catch the labeling in that quote?! *Lazy* and *irresponsible.* When our needs are not met, we blame others. In the NVC prayer, we work backwards from that—we are careful not to judge or label, and then we look inside ourselves to discover the unmet need causing our feelings.

To identify needs, especially women's needs, Rosenberg says something quite poignant:

> In a world where we're often judged harshly for identifying and revealing our needs, doing so can be very frightening. Women, in particular, are susceptible to criticism. For centuries, the image of the loving woman has been associated with sacrifice and the denial of one's own needs to take care of others. Because women are socialized to view the caretaking of others as their highest duty, they often learn to ignore their own needs.[107]

I related to this. When I first began practicing nonviolent communication and praying mightily using these steps, I often got stuck at this point. *What* actually did I need? I didn't know. I had never been taught to identify my needs before.

But as I wrestled with the Lord to apply this step in prayer, and intently searched my soul, I began to recognize my needs. And I started to put them into words.

Are you able to identify your needs? If this is challenging for you, don't give up. You can do it! Keep asking yourself, "What is the need at the root of this?" And follow your stream of thoughts. Then ask again, "But what is the need at the root of *that*?" And follow your stream of thoughts again! Ask again and again until you recognize the root. It will come to you and you will feel it. You will think, "Ah! *That* is what I need!"

Sometimes, we might think we know our needs ("I just need my kids to stop fighting!"), but often, there is a deeper need underneath. That is why it is important to ask again and again, "What is the need at the root of that?"

Looking at established lists of basic human needs can help you pinpoint what you need. Which need in the following list might be the underlying need to "I just need my husband to talk nicer to me?" Which need below might be the underlying one for "I need a friend to talk to?" Let's look at two well-known lists of needs.

Abraham Maslow's Hierarchy of Needs

In 1943, Abraham Maslow, an American psychologist, proposed a hierarchy of basic human needs. This list of needs can be found in a myriad of resources on the internet. A more in-depth discussion than what I offer below can be found at https://www.simplypsychology.org/maslow.html.

Over time, Maslow's list of needs has been added upon, but we will discuss his original five.

Maslow's Hierarchy of Needs

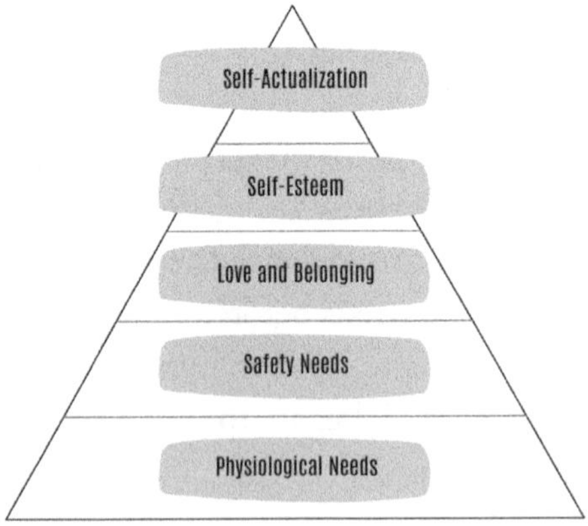

1. Psychological Needs

In a triangle displaying the importance of needs, Maslow placed physiological needs at the base of this model. These are biological requirements for human survival, such as food, water, oxygen, shelter, clothing, and sleep.

Perhaps as you walk through the steps of the NVC Prayer, you might get to this point and realize what you truly need is to fuel your body better. Or perhaps what you need is a good night of sleep (or two or three). Can you identify areas in your life right now where you could improve on your physiological needs?

2. Safety Needs

The next need on Maslow's hierarchy triangle is safety needs. Order, predictability, and control of our lives fall in this category: things such as consistent employment and financial security, family stability, and safety through law and order.

Are these needs being met? Are you concerned about financial matters? Does your life seem out of control? Do you need more stability and safety in a strained relationship? Can you identify your needs falling in this category?

3. Love and Belonging

Love and belonging are the third level up. These needs are met in relationships and are often the reason we seek connection. Belonging encompasses the emotional need to connect and be part of a group. This is fostered through interpersonal relationships.

At the root of your troubles, are you are feeling a lack of belonging and love? Do you feel lonely? Do you need to be seen and loved more?

4. Self-Esteem

The fourth level in Maslow's Hierarchy is esteem needs: self-worth, accomplishment, and respect. This includes both esteem for oneself (dignity, achievement, mastery, and independence) and the desire for others to give us high esteem (reputation, respect, status, prestige).

Ponder on your challenges. Do you need a sense of independence and freedom? Do you need colleagues or family members to respect you? Do you need to respect yourself?

5. Self-Actualization

The last and highest level in Maslow's triangle is self-actualization, which is the realization of a person's potential, self-fulfillment, and personal growth. This level is about the desire and need "to become everything one is capable of becoming."[108] This encapsulates one living their life calling.

Do you need to feel fulfilled? Do you need to nurture your God-given gifts? Are you hungering to fulfill what you were born to do?

Tony Robbins's Six Basic Human Needs

In recent years, Tony Robbins, an American author, coach, and philanthropist, adapted Maslow's theory and created his own list: The Six Basic Human Needs. Jennifer Price, a Christian and an international interventionist, summarizes these needs in her article, "The 6 Human Needs."[109] The following only briefly covers each need, in no particular order.

Robbins's List of Needs

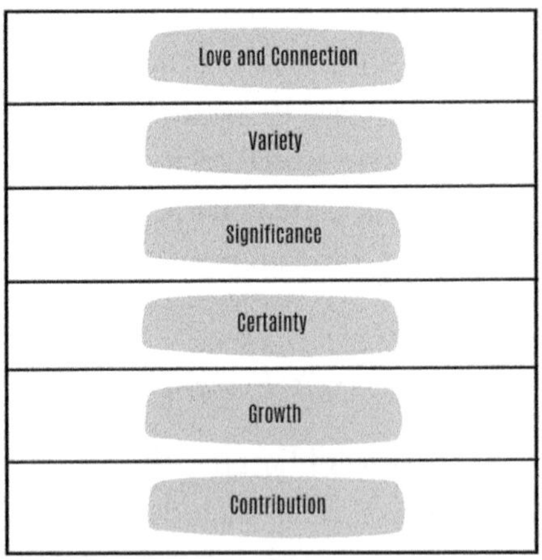

1. Love and Connection

Love and connection are the strong bonds and feelings of closeness and union with someone or something.

Think on the mighty prayer you are praying. Are you feeling a lack of love and connection in your life? Are you longing for love and connection in a rocky relationship? Is that what you truly need?

2. Variety

Variety is the need for change, for new stimuli. Though this might seem in opposition to Maslow's need for safety and consistency, variety plays an important role in our lives. "Variety exercises our emotional, psychological, mental, and physical range. Variety is one way to combat depression and anxiety. A good dose of variety is healthy and the excitement that ensues is necessary to feel alive."[110] For some, variety can mean eating at a new restaurant, for others, it means theme parks and exotic vacations.

Do you need more variety in your life? Are you feeling frustrated with people or things because this need is not being met? Do you need a change from the mundane daily grind?

3. Significance

Significance is the need to feel special, unique, or important. In small and large ways, we desire feeling needed and wanted. Without significance, we feel small and worthless.

Does this need resonate with you? Do you desire recognition and acknowledgement from your children? Or spouse? Parents? A boss? Perhaps the true need is that you need to believe in your own significance?

4. Certainty

Certainty is the need to feel safe, to be comfortable in your environment, and to experience pleasure while avoiding pain. When this need is unmet, we live in fear and can feel stable, grounded, protected, and secure.

Thinking on your life right now, is this need met? Do you need to tell the Lord, "I just need to feel safe and secure in this relationship with my father"? Or maybe, "I need to feel safe in my job"?

5. Growth

Growth is one of the last basic needs. This is the need for expansion of capacity, capability, and understanding. We need growth spiritually, intellectually, physically, and emotionally to have a healthy life.

Is this the underlying cause for the turmoil and wrestle you are experiencing? Do you feel suffocated in life and need to expand and grow? Do you feel stifled at work and need to be stimulated and given opportunities to progress?

6. Contribution

Contribution is a sense of service, of helping, giving, and supporting others. It is to look beyond oneself and to give to others with no expectation of personal gain. Price calls this the king of the six human needs because it encompasses all other needs. "If you focus on Contribution, you'll have Connection, and probably Love, with others while helping them. You'll have Variety as you're doing something different from your everyday routine. Significance is fulfilled because you know you're helping others, improving lives, making a difference. You'll have Certainty of being able to contribute. Growth occurs because anytime you contribute to others, you grow spiritually, mentally, emotionally/psychologically, and, if there's physical activity involved, you'll grow physically."[111] Perhaps this is why the Church puts so much focus and energy on service. They have a humanitarian program that allows volunteers to provide aid worldwide, occasional youth nights and ward activities focused on service, and a directory website of local service opportunities (justserve.org) that helps individuals fulfill this need.

Ask yourself if this need for contribution is unmet in your life. Are you feeling a desire to help others and serve? Is this at the root of your struggles?

If I think, "I need more money," I find it very helpful to look at these lists and consider what need it falls under. It is empowering to recognize more money might actually mean I feel my need for safety is not being met. Saying, "I need to feel financially safe and secure," resonates with me. ("Yes! That is what I need right now!") And that is what I will tell Heavenly Father.

Perhaps, I think, "I just need a break from life." What need might this fall under on these lists? Variety—a break from the daily grind? Recognition—to be seen and acknowledged for the daily efforts that go unseen? Physiological—a nap? Use the above list to pinpoint your underlying need. It might surprise you what you learn about yourself!

In my younger days, I erroneously expected other human beings to meet my needs. When I felt unseen, unnoticed, unimportant, or like I didn't belong, I wondered who would help me feel seen and important. Where did I belong? Who would fill my need for connection?

I relied on the people in my life to fulfill these needs in me—my husband, my parents, my friends, Church leaders . . . everyone. And it was massively devastating when I realized they were incapable of fully meeting my needs. I spent many painful long hours and days wondering how I could find peace and solace in this life if my needs were not met.

As I began practicing the NVC Prayer, I started to see my needs could be met without any changes in my outer environment. No one in my life needed to change their behavior or actions, and yet it was still possible for my needs to be met.

Approach the Lord in prayer. Observe your situations, express your feelings, and then discover your deepest needs to learn what I have. I am excited for the expanded growth and understanding you will receive!

Our subconscious makes every effort to meet our needs. It is a matter of survival for us. I realized, profoundly, that Satan knows this, and *he works really hard to meet our needs in his own way.* If he can make us believe that his way is the fastest, best, and easiest way to meet our needs, we might succumb to temptation. If we hold strong and remember that God can meet our needs—and will—and pray to Him, we can withstand temptation. I imagine a time when everyone solely relies on Heavenly Father to meet their needs and Satan is paid no mind. That time is when Satan will be bound by our own agency and choice to turn to the Lord.

That will be a beautiful time. We can prepare for it now.

Step 4: Request

Finally, after we have observed, expressed, and stated our need to God, we request His help. In this step of our prayer, we ask distinctly and clearly what we wish He would do to meet our need. We are requesting our kind and loving Father in Heaven for help.

I recently participated in an online self-paced course called 21 Days of Prayer to Change Your Life through the Daily OM website. Angela Montano, the instructor, is not a member of The Church of Jesus Christ of Latter-day Saints, so her thinking around prayer and the way she prayed was different than what I was used to. I enjoyed the new perspective. She writes, "Prayer bridges the gap between our vulnerability and our greater power. . . . It is our capacity to reach beyond our limited sense of self and possibility. Prayer is a healing energy that we can use all day long, every day."[112] This bridge of prayer becomes healing balm when we are able to ask Heavenly Father for the help we need.

Our ability to request help from the God of the Universe amazes me. In her course, Montano taught the acronym HELP and introduced the words "Hello Eternal Loving Presence."[113] I liked this idea—that we are requesting help from our Father, an Eternal Loving Presence. This reminded me that He *is* an eternal presence, and a loving presence, and an eternal loving presence in my life. He cares about me. And He cares about you—He is an Eternal Loving Presence in your life as well. He desires that we request what we need from Him so that He can reach out and help us.

Rosenberg suggests ways to make clear requests. He says we want to "word our requests in the form of concrete actions . . . and to avoid vague, abstract, or ambiguous phrasing."[114] We want to be as specific as possible in the request. This might sound like I am suggesting you ask Heavenly Father to bless you with a red Lamborghini or tickets to Jamaica. However, think of step three in the NVC prayer and realize that, most likely, a physical object is not what we are needing. Instead, we are asking for assistance in shifting how we feel, a change in our perspective, or additional knowledge and understanding.

Returning to the previous need, "I need more money," which we learned could mean a desire to feel more secure and safe, I could request Divine assistance by asking, "Heavenly Father, wilt Thou help me feel safe and secure?" And if you think about it—which prayer can be answered faster? A feeling can change in moments, when monetary increase involves other people, more time, and many other circumstances all coming together. Changing the way we feel can change our circumstances.

Or perhaps the need you are taking to God is based on a painful relationship where you are desiring connection. You can request to feel more connection. "Heavenly Father, wilt Thou help me feel loved and like I belong? Wilt Thou help me feel connection in this relationship with so-and-so?" Maybe it is *you* who wants to help meet someone else's need. "Wilt Thou help me show love to my daughter and help her feel like she belongs amongst members of the Church?" Walking through the NVC Prayer process and then humbly asking for help brings enlightenment and shows Him your heart's desire.

This final step of the prayer is a moment of vulnerability and humility. Steps one through three prepared your heart and helped you see more clearly. Now, you have been humbled and brought to the understanding that you need help, and you need it in a specific way from Heavenly Father and Jesus Christ. Making a direct request allows Heavenly Father to answer and invites the Savior to assist in His specific and personalized way.

This step could be difficult as we might think, "I just need my father to change so I am requesting that he stop being a narcissist." Or, "I need my son to return to the gospel path so I'm requesting he come back to church." But Heavenly Father honors agency, so the request you make must honor others' agency as well. If you find yourself requesting actions of others to change, then return to step three and discover what need is not being met by their actions. Once you have determined this, you can request the need of feeling love regardless of how your father treats you, or feeling peace and hope even if your son doesn't return to the gospel path in this life. You can request your need to be met by the Eternal Loving Presence in your life, and still honor and respect others' agency.

When I have prayed the NVC Prayer, I have felt Heavenly Father's presence in a way I don't feel at other times. It is like His presence is near me, words and thoughts in my mind sound differently than my own, and my understanding is expanded. My relationship has grown with Him. As I put in effort, wrestling with my own judgments, assumptions, and evaluations, I feel heard and seen. And I receive answers in sacred, private ways. My Father knows me, and He listens to my heartfelt prayers. I know He knows you and desires a relationship with you. I wonder what experiences you will have as you explore your relationship with Him through the NVC Prayer.

NVC Prayer Examples

As mentioned earlier, I attended a training in England. There were ten of us present for the week. We were all from different countries, backgrounds, and religions, and yet, we came together and had an extraordinary experience creating a space of belonging, friendship, and love.

Recently, I missed them. Though I am surrounded by wonderful friends here at home, I was longing for the closeness we felt with each other. I missed feeling seen and heard. I ached for the belonging I had felt.

Here is an example of how I would use the NVC Prayer in this situation. See if you can identify the observation, feeling, need, and request.

> Heavenly Father, while I was in England, I was surrounded by friends every hour of the day. We shared a cottage, we ate breakfast, we went on forest therapy walks, we talked about our nature experiences, we ate lunch and dinner, and we spent evenings together talking about our lives and learnings.
>
> Here at home, I am bustling around with responsibilities. Yesterday, I cared for my sick teenage daughter who stayed home from school, and then I went to my chiropractic appointment. I made lunch for my daughter and two sons (who are very young). I put my youngest down for a nap. I got groceries, made dinner, waited for two daughters and my husband to get home from track practice so they could eat and I could clean up dinner, and then I went to bed early and very tired.
>
> I am feeling sad. I am feeling sad for the connection I had with my friends, during the training, that I don't have

> now. I'm also feeling sad for the loss of the slow-paced days I lived while away, for the ability to be present and feel peace and calm. I am feeling frustrated that I can't merge the busyness of life and my responsibilities with being present in the relationships I have with others around me.

I pause now and wonder to myself . . . *Hmm. What do I* really *need?* As I open my heart through my observations and my feelings, I realize there is not just one need here. I need connection, but I also need less busyness. I need greater calm and peace in my life and a foundation of certainty. I need to feel seen and heard and important to someone. I need to feel significant.

When I scan these thoughts, the one that really sinks deep and resonates with me is the need for connection. So, for now, I will address that need in my prayer.

"Heavenly Father, I need connection in my life. The connections were so strong and felt so good in England. I miss that and need a little of it now in my life.

"Wilt Thou show me how to feel connection in my life?"

Then, as I go throughout my day, I will watch for the ways He shows me how to feel connected.

I could have asked, "Wilt Thou help me to feel connection?" or "Wilt Thou bless me to feel connected?" But in this moment, I wanted to empower myself and ask what I could do to meet the need I had.

Here is another example of an NVC prayer:

> Heavenly Father, my lower back burns and aches. When I bend over or stand up, it hurts. When I carried the groceries in yesterday, it hurt. When I mop, it hurts. I even iced it this morning, and it still hurts.
>
> I feel discouraged. I am discouraged because I have things I need to do that I can't finish because of the pain. I'm also frustrated about that. How can I be a good spouse and parent if I can't care for others because I'm in so much pain? I'm really frustrated at my lack of ability to do things. But mostly, I'm discouraged. And I even feel depressed. I'm sinking into depression because of this pain.

> I need the pain to be gone. I need to be able to do the things I need to do. I need to fulfill my responsibilities without pain. I need to feel safe in my body, that it won't 'betray' me when I rely on it. Yes. That's it. I need to feel safe in my body.
>
> Wilt Thou help me feel safe in my body? Wilt Thou tell me what to do to feel safe in my body?

Can you see how following your thoughts can help you explore different angles of your situation until you find the root of what you need? This heartfelt investigation *is* a mighty prayer! It is an investment of heart and soul, far more than the mere "please bless me to have friends" or "please help my back to feel better." This process shows Heavenly Father how much you desire His help and how much you are willing to work to get it. Because this is work! This is a powerful and revealing work.

Conclusion

This book offers ten prayers to help you pray more mightily:

1. The Appreciation Prayer
2. The What Prayer
3. The Eternal Gratitude Prayer
4. The Image Prayer
5. the Five-Year Prayer
6. The Pulse Prayer
7. The Because Prayer
8. The Music Prayer
9. The Mindful Blessing Prayer
10. The the Nonviolent Communication Prayer

However, this suggested list of mighty prayers is not conclusive. In what ways have you learned to pray mighty prayers? I'd love to know! Please email me your stories to Brittney.barney@gmail.com.

Becoming a mighty pray-er sets into motion great things, but choosing to become one can only be accomplished by one person—YOU! You must make the choice and use your agency to begin this process. Heighten your awareness of your physical senses, try out some of these prayer and ideas, and set the intent to look for the answers to your mighty prayers and watch the blessings that come from becoming a mighty pray-er. How will your relationship with Heavenly Father change as you do?

Epilogue

Can you have an epilogue to a nonfiction book? No matter. I am doing it.

The purpose of this book is to give ideas on how to pray more wholly with your heart, mind, and body. But in my recent personal study of the Atonement of Jesus Christ, the Spirit bore testimony to me that Jesus Christ *truly* has the ability to succor us in our times of need—and in our needs. He doesn't just have the ability, but *He knows how.* He knows exactly how to succor you because He experienced your unmet needs exactly as you are experiencing them, right now.

The Book of Mormon prophet Alma prophesied, "And he will take upon him their infirmities, that his bowels may be filled with mercy, according to the flesh, that he may know according to the flesh how to succor his people according to their infirmities."[115] He took upon Himself *your* infirmities, and He knows how to succor *you* according to your infirmities. President James E. Faust said, "The Savior has suffered anything and everything that we could ever feel or experience."[116]

Isaiah, an ancient prophet from the Old Testament, prophesied that the Savior would bear our griefs and our sorrows.[117] And He did! The Savior did that in the Garden of Gethsemane. Dallin H. Oaks said, "He therefore knows our struggles, our heartaches, our temptations, and our suffering, for He willingly experienced them all as an essential part of His Atonement. And because of this, His Atonement empowers Him to succor us—to give us the strength to bear it all."[118] The Psalmist beautifully bears testimony of this: "Many are the afflictions of the righteous: but the Lord delivereth him out of them all."[119]

Succoring His brothers and sisters is one of the Savior's life callings. Jesus Christ Himself proclaimed this as his mission at the very beginning of His ministry on the earth, that He was "sent to heal the brokenhearted."[120]

The question is, how often do we sit in our sorrows, our needs, and our broken hearts, and wait for the Savior to come to us? Is there a way to call forth this succoring power? I believe that is the power of the mighty prayer.

I believe we can talk to our Father in Heaven and share our hearts with Him in a myriad of ways—and then He allows our Brother to fulfill His life calling by succoring us. President Oaks says, "Because of His atoning experience in mortality, our Savior is able to comfort, heal, and strengthen all men and women everywhere, but I believe He does so *only for those who seek Him and ask for His help.*" He reaffirms, "We have only to ask."[121]

I truly believe a mighty prayer accesses the Atonement of Jesus Christ. It is reaching out with our thoughts, words, feelings, desires, and energy to accept the power of His Atonement. A mighty prayer seeks this power of succoring available only through the Atonement of Jesus Christ.

The scriptures bear testimony of this as well. In the New Testament Jesus says, "Ask, and it shall be given you; seek, and ye shall find; knock, and it shall be opened unto you"[122] And from the Doctrine and Covenants we learn: "Therefore, if you will ask of me you shall receive; if you will knock it shall be opened unto you."[123]

"The healing and strengthening power of Jesus Christ and His Atonement is for all of us who will ask."[124] (*We have only to ask.* Employ mighty prayer and access the power of the Atonement of Jesus Christ in your life.)

Perhaps this power will allow you to shift your perspective on your needs or meet your need differently than you have thought before. Perhaps accessing the power will allow you to see your situation more clearly, which will bring understanding and peace. "Sometimes He succors or helps by giving us the strength or patience to endure our infirmities."[125] The beauty of this is that "when the Savior knows you truly want to reach up to Him—when He can feel the greatest desire of your heart is to draw His power into your life—you will be led by the Holy Ghost to know exactly what you should do."[126]

This has been my experience, not just once, but many times. When I am intentional in mighty prayer, I am swiftly succored in my needs. I know this can be your experience too because the Savior loves *you*. He wants and waits to succor you. Heavenly Father and Jesus Christ do not desire that you suffer. They care about you. They love you. They desire you to become a mighty pray-er.

You can do it.

Endnotes

1. David A. Bednar, "Pray Always," *Ensign*, Nov. 2008.
2. Gordon B. Hinckley, *Teachings of Gordon B. Hinckley* (Deseret Book, 1997), 114.
3. Alma 58:10–11; emphasis added.
4. Joseph Smith—History 1:1–29.
5. *A Year of Powerful Prayer: Getting Answers for Your Every Day* (Deseret Book, 2013), 35.
6. 1 Nephi 1:5.
7. 1 Nephi 1:6.
8. Enos 1:11–12.
9. Enos 1:17.
10. Alma 8:10.
11. Jacob Z. Hess, Carrie Skarda, Kyle Anderson, and Ty Mansfield, *The Power of Stillness: Mindful Living for Latter-day Saints* (Deseret Book, 2019), 53.
12. Callie Jeppson, email message to author, Feb. 9, 2025.
13. Elise Tarango, "Prophetic Heart Healing Training," Online Course, accessed July 2023, prophetichearthealing.com.
14. Bednar, "Pray Always."
15. Mary Jane Woodger, "What I Have Learned about Mighty Prayer," *Ensign*, Dec. 2006.
16. Angela Montano, email message to author, Dec. 17, 2023.
17. "What Is the Circle of Security?" accessed February 7, 2025, https://www.circleofsecurityinternational.com/circle-of-security-model/what-is-the-circle-of-security/.
18. Ibid.
19. Doctrine and Covenants 4:2.
20. *A Year of Powerful Prayer.*
21. Tarango, "Heart Healing."
22. Russell M. Nelson, "Hear Him," *Ensign*, May 2020.
23. Tarango, "Heart Healing."
24. David Butler, *Spirit: The Gift That Connects You to Heaven* (Deseret Book, 2020) 36.
25. Jessica Garner, email message to author, Oct. 25, 2023.
26. Alexander Dushku, "Pillars and Rays," *Liahona*, May 2024.
27. Allie Duzett, "What if I Can't Hear Divine Guidance," Youtube, March 4, 2022, https://www.youtube.com/watch?v=rMfXz4vfrPU&ab_channel=AllieDuzett%3AMEDICALINTUITIVE).
28. Butler, *Spirit*, 36.
29. Allie Duzett, "What if I Can't Hear Divine Guidance," Youtube, March 4, 2022, https://www.youtube.com/watch?v=rMfXz4vfrPU&ab_channel=AllieDuzett%3AMEDICALINTUITIVE).
30. Richard G. Scott, "To Acquire Spiritual Guidance," *Ensign*, Nov. 2009.
31. Hank R. Smith, Commentary on Inspirational Quote, Facebook, December, 13 2022, https://www.facebook.com/photo/?fbid=735952157892372&set=a.289886765832249&paipv=0&eav=AfZOTraA23HERmqlAmP4b23L56BFKZahRLjz25TzWkltoAIAYqFBDkLjqImX3rg3ND4&_rdr.
32. Jacob Z. Hess, Carrie Skarda, Kyle Anderson, and Ty Mansfield, *The Power of Stillness: Mindful Living for Latter-day Saints* (Deseret Book, 2019), 43.
33. Hess, *Stillness*, 62.
34. Ibid., *Stillness*, 8.
35. Ibid., *Stillness*, 60.
36. Joy D. Jones, "An Especially Noble Calling," *Ensign*, May 2020.
37. Enos 1:11–12.
38. Angie Asplund (@healthful_dwelling), "Heaven's Answers," Instagram, August 12, 2023, https://www.instagram.com/p/Cv2UoY7LXPx/?img_index=1.
39. Ibid.

40. Emily Robison Adams, *Divine Quietness: Finding Meaning when Heaven Is Silent,* (Deseret Book, 2023), 24.
41. Adams, *Divine Quietness,* 43.
42. Ibid., 39.
43. Ibid., 44.
44. Tracy Y. Browning, "Seeking Answers to Spiritual Questions," *Ensign*, Nov. 2025.
45. Psalm 27:14.
46. Ibid.
47. Paul W. Reeve, *Let's Talk About Race and Priesthood* (Deseret Book, 2023), 112.
48. Intuitive Healing with Allie Duzett, "Unhealthy Beliefs about Prayers Post," Facebook, December 7, 2023, https:www.facebook.com/groups/1514390408801404/search/?q=brittney%20barney.
49. Mosiah 27:26.
50. "I Pray in Faith," *Children's Songbook,* 14.
51. John 11:41.
52. Tarango, "Heart Healing."
53. Sungshim Loppnow, "Relational Circuits (RCs)—An Introduction to a Vital Tool," Loppnow Relationship Center, January 18, 2021, https://www.loppnowrelationship-center.com/blog/relational-circuits.
54. Melissa Romano, "Vagus Nerve Toolkit," The Vagus Nerve Miracle Course, DailyOM, https://courses.dailyom.com/courses/take/1140/texts/44702656–vagus-nerve-toolkit. Accessed Nov 15 2023.
55. Romano, "Vagus Nerve."
56. Loppnow, "Relational Circuits."
57. Bible Dictionary, "Emmanuel."
58. 1 Thessalonians 5:18.
59. Joseph Smith—History 1:10.
60. Joseph Smith—History 1:18; emphasis added.
61. Acts 9:6.
62. Nancy Crawford, email message to author, Feb. 7, 2025.
63. Scott, "Spiritual Guidance."
64. Allie Duzett, "Healing Your Boundaries" Group Session, Allieduzettclasses.com, www.allieduzettclasses.com/products/courses/view/1157832. Accessed 2023.
65. Alma 40:8.
66. Doctrine and Covenants 130:7; emphasis added.
67. Bednar, "Pray Always."
68. Proverbs 22:6.
69. Doctrine and Covenants 6:36.
70. 2 Corinthians 4:17.
71. Jessica Garner, email message to author, Aug. 31, 2023.
72. 2 Corinthians 6:10.
73. Caroline Myss and Dr. Norm Shealy, "The Holographic View and Guided Imagery for working with the Body, Attitudes, and Emotions: Part 1," The Science of Medical Intuition Course, Sounds True, https://elearning.soundstrue.com/courses/take/the-science-of-medical-intuition-self-diagnosis-and-healing-within-your-body-s-energy-systems/texts/10288822–the-holographic-view-and-guided-imagery-for-working-with-the-body-attitudes-and-emotions-part-one. Accessed 18 Nov 2023.
74. Ibid.
75. Asplund, "Heaven's Answers."
76. Moses 6:27.
77. Doctrine and Covenants 42:49.
78. Allie Duzett, "Number One Thing to do to Prepare for the Future," Youtube, Mar. 3, 2022, https://www.youtube.com/watch?v=huNCIP_ZQ50&ab_channel=Allieduzett%3AMEDICALINTUITIVE.
79. Hinckley, 109.
80. Duzett, "Number One."

81. Psalm 43:3.
82. Duzett, "Number One."
83. Psalm 4:4.
84. David Bowman, "Drawn In," https://www.davidbowmanart.com/pages/engaging-the-entire-family-in-come-follow-me.
85. John 11:41.
86. Matthew 6:9.
87. Hillsong United, "Know You Will," https://www.worshiptogether.com/songs/know-you-will-hillsong-united/.
88. Doctrine and Covenants 25:12.
89. Henri Rand Furgiuele, "Food, Food, Food," Quantum-Touch, https://quantumtouch.com/en/about-us/articles/2686–food-food-food, November 18, 2023.
90. Oren Jay Sofer, *Say What You Mean* (Shambhala Publications, 2018), 170.
91. "OBSERVE | Meaning in the Cambridge English Dictionary." n.d. Dictionary.cambridge.org. https://dictionary.cambridge.org/dictionary/english/observe.
92. Sofer, *Say What,* 172.
93. Marshall B. Rosenberg, *Nonviolent Communication: A Language of Life* (PuddleDancer Press, 2015), 26.
94. Sofer, *Say What,* 173.
95. Ibid., 174.
96. Ibid.,*Say What,* 173.
97. Basil Barney, "Onions" (in author's possession, 2020).
98. Sofer, *Say What,* 174.
99. Ibid., 180.
100. Rosenberg, *Nonviolent Communication,* 41.
101. Ibid., *Nonviolent Communication,* 41.
102. Matthew 7:1.
103. Rosenberg, *Nonviolent Communication,* 49.
104. Ibid., *Nonviolent Communication,* 50.
105. Ibid., *Nonviolent Communication,* 49.
106. Ibid., *Nonviolent Communication,* 53.
107. Ibid., *Nonviolent Communication,* 55.
108. Saul McLeod, "Maslow's Hierarchy of Needs," accessed April 17, 2025, https://www.simplypsychology.org/maslow.html.
109. Jennifer Price, "The 6 Human Needs," accessed April 17, 2025, https://barriefht.ca/wp-content/uploads/2021/01/The-6-Human-Needs.pdf.
110. Ibid.
111. Ibid.
112. Angela Montano, email message to author, Dec. 17, 2023.
113. Angela Montano, "The Strength in Vulnerability," *21 Days of Prayer to Change Your Life,* Daily OM, www.courses.dailyom.com/courses/take/813/texts/39847316–the-strength-in-vulnerability. Accessed December 23, 2023.
114. Rosenberg, *Nonviolent Communication,* 69.
115. Alma 7:12.
116. James E. Faust, "The Atonement: Our Greatest Hope," *Ensign,* Nov. 2001.
117. Isaiah 53:4.
118. Dallin H. Oaks, "Strengthened by the Atonement," *Ensign*, Nov. 2015.
119. Psalm 34:19.
120. Luke 4:18.
121. Oaks, "Strengthened by the Atonement."
122. Matthew 7:7.
123. Doctrine and Covenants 6:5.
124. Oaks, "Strengthened by the Atonement."
125. Ibid.
126. Russell M. Nelson, "Drawing the Power of Jesus Christ into Our Lives," *Ensign,* May 2017.

About the Author

Brittney Barney is a certified forest therapy guide, trained in mindful awareness in nature and every-day living. She enjoys experimenting with mindful practices and communication strategies in prayer to improve her relationship with Heavenly Father and Jesus Christ.

She loves to create—stories, food, music, and pine needle baskets. She even published a Bible-based collaborative card game called Escaping Egypt. She has an obsession with birds, healthy eating, and learning to play musical instruments. She currently teaches music to preschoolers up to middle schoolers, and enjoys conducting her middle school band and orchestra classes. She is married to a trademark attorney, has five daughters and two sons, and resides in Washington.

BECOMING

ENCOUNTERING THE LORD

A MIGHTY

WITH ALL YOUR SENSES

PRAY-ER

BECOMING

ENCOUNTERING THE LORD

A MIGHTY

WITH ALL YOUR SENSES

PRAY-ER

BRITTNEY BARNEY

CFI
An imprint of Cedar Fort, Inc.
Springville, Utah

Paperback ISBN 13: 978-1-4621-4981-0
eBook ISBN 13: 978-1-4621-4982-7

Published by CFI, an imprint of Cedar Fort, Inc.
2373 W. 700 S., Suite 100, Springville, UT 84663
Distributed by Cedar Fort, Inc., www.cedarfort.com

Library of Congress Cataloging Number: 2025938888

Cover design by Shawnda Craig

Printed in the United States of America

10 9 8 7 6 5 4 3 2 1

Printed on acid-free paper